Finger Food

Finger Food

DELECTABLE DIPS,
NIBBLES AND BITES
FOR PERFECT PARTIES

Elizabeth Wolf-Cohen

Photography by
Amanda Heywood

southwater

This edition is published by Southwater

Distributed in the UK by
The Manning Partnership
251–253 London Road East
Batheaston
Bath BA1 7RL
tel. 01225 852 727
fax 01225 852 852

Published in the USA by
Anness Publishing Inc.
27 West 20th Street
Suite 504
New York
NY 10011
fax 212 807 6813

Distributed in Canada by
General Publishing
895 Don Mills Road
400–402 Park Centre
Toronto, Ontario M3C 1W3
tel. 416 445 3333
fax 416 445 5991

Distributed in Australia by
Sandstone Publishing
Unit 1, 360 Norton Street
Leichhardt
New South Wales 2040
tel. 02 9560 7888
fax 02 9560 7488

Southwater is an imprint of Anness Publishing Limited
Hermes House, 88–89 Blackfriars Road, London SE1 8HA
tel. 020 7401 2077; fax 020 7633 9499

© 1995, 2001 Anness Publishing Limited

Publisher: Joanna Lorenz
Project Editor: Joanne Rippin
Designer: Alan Marshall
Jacket design: The Bridgewater Book Company Limited
Photographers: Amanda Heywood
Production Controller: Joanna King

MEASUREMENTS

Three sets of measurements have been provided in the recipes here,
in the following order: Metric, Imperial and American. It is essential that
units of measurements are not mixed within each recipe. Where
conversions result in awkward numbers, these have been rounded
for convenience, but are accurate enough to produce successful results.

Previously published as *Step-by-Step 50 Party Pieces*

3 5 7 9 10 8 6 4 2

CONTENTS

INTRODUCTION

A party is the perfect way to show off some of the prettiest and tastiest foods. And, because most of the preparation work can be done in advance, this kind of entertaining is generally much less demanding than formal dinner parties.

Planning the menu is the most enjoyable part of the preparations – informal or formal, large or small, close friends or business associates, the occasion will help you decide the right scale and approach. Time of day and the length of your guests' stay will also influence your arrangements – a few drinks with friends before going to a film will require only one or two nibbles, whereas a three-hour party after a family Christening will obviously need something rather more substantial.

Small pieces of food that can be eaten with one hand make the best party foods (remember that each guest will be holding a glass in one hand). Plan to have something to serve the moment people arrive, maybe a tray of crudités with a dip, as this gives guests something to focus on and helps them to relax. Move on to something hot when most people have arrived, then alternate between hot and cold, finishing with something warm or sweet. Serving sweet food is an ideal, subtle way of suggesting that the party is drawing to a close.

In this book, you will find easy recipes for simple roasted nuts and herbed olives, as well as more elaborate concoctions, such as wild rice pancakes with smoked salmon nests. But remember, with a little imagination almost any food can be adapted to a party-sized piece.

Condiments

Many different condiments can be used to put together a quick dip or snack at a moment's notice. Tomato ketchup and horseradish sauce can be stirred together with mayonnaise and a squeeze of lemon, to use as a dip for prawns or hard-boiled eggs. Or add chopped spring onion to soy sauce and mango chutney and spoon on to prawn crackers for another instant snack. The variations are endless – just use your imagination.

Barbecue sauce
Bottled barbecue sauces are ideal for adding an outdoor flavour to quick grills. They can be used to spread on pieces of meat or vegetables, then grilled and skewered onto a cocktail stick.

Capers
The little buds of the Mediterranean caper bush, preserved in vinegar, will add an extra piquancy to sauces and salads. They are especially good on pizzas and salads.

Chilli sauce
This bottled sauce is widely available in supermarkets and Chinese grocers. It gives a warm sweet-spicy tingle to most foods and sauces. Use in dips and marinades.

Dijon mustard
Indispensable for salad dressings, sauces and dips, as well as to spread on meats and cheeses. It is sometimes flavoured with green peppercorns or other aromatics.

English mustard
Sold ready-made or as powder to be mixed to a paste. This is the traditional relish for accompanying beef, ham and cheese.

Grainy mustard
The best known grainy mustard is from the region near Meaux, France, though English traditional whole-grain mustards are also available. It is delicious with ham and pâtés.

Horseradish sauce
This hot spicy sauce can be bought as a relish, or "creamed" which makes it slightly milder. Perfect with beef, smoked and oily fish, chicken and seafood.

Mango chutney
Delicious with cheese or ham, or stirred into chicken mayonnaise, egg mayonnaise or diced lamb.

Mayonnaise
A good-quality mayonnaise is indispensable. Use as a dip or a spread or to bind chopped hard-boiled eggs or chicken into toppings for toasts to serve as a quick canapé. Making your own is worth the effort.

Plum sauce
Made from plums, apricots, garlic, chillies, sugar, vinegar and flavourings, this thick, sweet Cantonese condiment makes an ideal dip for Chinese-style snacks, or base for a barbecue sauce.

Soy sauce
This sauce is the basis of many Chinese-style dips and sauces. (Light soy sauce is more common than dark, but it is more salty. Dilute it with a little water.) Add chopped spring onions and coriander for an easy dipping sauce.

Sweetcorn relish
This sweet and tangy relish for hamburgers can also be used to top slices of cold chicken, beef or ham or hard-boiled eggs.

Tartare sauce
This is the standard sauce for fried fish and seafood. It is delicious with fish cakes. A mixture of mayonnaise, sweet gherkins, spring onions, capers and vinegar; try making your own.

Tomato chutney
Chutneys of all kinds make a tasty accompaniment to cold meats and salamis as well as cheeses and cold grilled vegetables.

Tomato ketchup
This universal condiment can be used in barbecue sauces and marinades or spread on toast and top with cheese or meats for a quick canapé.

capers
barbecue sauce
chilli sauce
plum sauce
soy sauce
horseradish sauce
mango chutney
tartare sauce
sweetcorn relish
tomato ketchup
mayonnaise
Dijon mustard
tomato chutney
English mustard
grainy mustard

Herbs

Fresh herbs can be used generously in party foods, as they provide fresh flavour and interest to many different dishes. They also make a simple but elegant garnish. Use the same herb that you use in a recipe to garnish the serving plate – this provides a hint of what's in the food.

If you are lucky enough to have a garden, or even a window-box, grow your own herbs so you will always have some to hand. If you can't grow your own, choose from the extensive range of fresh herbs now available from supermarkets.

flat-leaf parsley
mint
bay
watercress
lemon grass
thyme
chives
dill
oregano
basil
coriander

Basil
The warm, spicy scent of basil epitomizes the flavours of the Mediterranean. Use it with tomatoes, summer salad, vegetable dishes and of course in pesto with pine nuts and Parmesan cheese.

Bay
This leaf of the laurel family gives a delicate flavour to soups, casseroles and pâtés. Bay leaves make a pretty garnish which will stay fresh for hours.

Chives
A member of the onion family, the mild flavour is wonderful with almost anything, but especially in herb butters, cheeses, cream sauces, egg dishes and of course with sour cream on jacket potatoes.

Coriander
This wonderfully aromatic herb is used in Mexican, Chinese, Indian, Greek, Turkish and North African cooking, to add subtle spiciness to dishes such as stir-fries, curries and hummus.

Dill
Most often used in fish dishes such as the Scandinavian *gravlax*, the slightly aniseed flavour of dill is also delicious with eggs, potatoes, chicken and cucumber and soft cheese recipes. Its soft fernlike leaves make a lovely garnish.

Flat-leaf parsley
Sometimes called Italian or Continental parsley, this variety has a slightly stronger flavour than curly parsley. It adds interest and colour to almost any savoury dish, especially vegetables and fish, and makes a beautiful garnish.

Lemon grass
The stem of this lemon-scented, broad-leaved grass is used in South East Asian dishes, especially those from Thailand. If you cannot find it, substitute a little freshly grated lemon zest.

Mint
This herb, with its many varieties, gives a fresh tingle to fish, goat's cheeses, salads and is wonderful in dips. It is used extensively in Middle Eastern cooking.

Oregano
Sometimes called wild majoram, it has a powerful flavour used in tomato sauces and with vegetable dishes of the Southern Mediterranean and Greece.

Thyme
This intensely aromatic herb is used in lamb or chicken dishes. It is also good in tomato sauces and vegetable dishes and is an integral part of a bouquet garni.

Watercress
Technically, this is a vegetable and a member of the mustard family. Its peppery flavour is particularly good in sandwiches or with egg and fish and it can be used as an attractive garnish.

Spices

Spices are an important part of all kinds of cooking, but are especially useful in party food to provide extra flavour and stimulate the appetite. Store all spices, ground or whole, in air-tight jars, away from heat or light, to prevent loss of colour and flavour. If possible grind your own freshly each time, especially pepper and nutmeg.

Aniseed
This Mediterranean seed is used in breads and pastries, as well as in fish dishes and marinades.

Cardamom pods
Used in Indian, Arab and North African stews and other dishes, the sweetish fragrant flavour is also popular in German and Scandinavian baking. Crush the pods with a rolling pin to release the flavour. Cardamom is also available ready-ground, but in this form loses its flavour quickly.

Cayenne pepper
This is the ground red powder of a very pungent dried red chilli. It can be used sparingly in a variety of dishes and sauces to add piquancy and warmth. It has the advantage of being virtually invisible.

Chilli flakes
These flakes are crushed hot, red chillies and include pieces of the chillies as well as the seeds. They are very strong but, used sparingly, make an ideal addition to soups, stews, marinades, and sauces.

Cinnamon
Available in sticks or powdered, its warm flavour is well known in baking. The sticks can also be used in spicy meat or vegetable stews and in poaching syrups for fruits and in custards.

Coriander seeds
The small round seeds of the coriander plant have a warm, mildly spicy flavour when roasted. They are used in Indian, Moroccan and South East Asian cooking as well as in pickling and marinades.

Cumin
This mildly piquant seed has a sweetish flavour and intense aroma. Used in many North African dishes, it can be bought as seeds or ready-ground.

Dried mustard powder
This is the traditional English mustard, based on ground brown and white mustard seeds. Mixed to a paste with cold water, vinegar or milk, it is the traditional accompaniment for beef, ham and cheeses. The strong but smooth pungent flavour is ideal for fish, egg and vegetable dishes, as well as many sauces.

Dried root ginger
This can be grated into many dishes to give a hot and spicy, yet refreshing, flavour. Fresh root ginger can replace dried if peeled and then chopped or grated finely. Delicious in many Chinese, Indian and Middle Eastern dishes.

Fennel seeds
The seeds of the fennel bulb have a sweet, aniseed flavour. They can be used in baking and to flavour soups and stews. They can also be used instead of aniseed.

Fresh chillies
Technically, chillies are a vegetable from the capsicum family. Used sparingly they add a lively heat to all kinds of dishes, especially curries and salsas.

Garlic
Technically a member of the onion family, garlic is most often used as a flavouring, although fresh sweet garlic can also be cooked as a vegetable. In small quantities, its sweet, pungent flavour enhances almost any savoury dish.

Hot red chillies
These small, intensely hot chillies are frequently used in many Thai and other South East Asian dishes. Use sparingly.

Mustard seeds
The seeds of the mustard plant impart a hot pungent taste and aroma to any marinade or pickled dish. Crush lightly to release the flavour.

Nutmeg
Besides being a baking essential, a little freshly grated nutmeg adds a warm, sweet, nutty flavour to pastas, white sauces, and cheese dishes.

Paprika
This red powder, ground from dried ripe capsicums, can be mild or hot. It is used in Austrian and Hungarian cooking as well as in many Spanish dishes. It can be used as a pretty garnish on egg dishes, or creamy sauces.

Peppercorns
Green peppercorns are the unripe fruit of the *Piper nigrum* vine. They have a milder flavour than the black peppercorns, which are small pickled green peppercorns, dried whole. One of the most important spices, freshly ground black pepper is intensely aromatic and mildly spicy.

Poppy seeds
The tiny, hard slate-blue seeds of the opium poppy are used mostly in baking. Try them in salad dressings and noodle dishes for a slightly sweet, nutty flavour.

Sea salt
The large white crystals of dried sea salt have a pure salty flavour and can be used in cooking or on the table. Try using sea salt as a dip for quail's eggs or sprinkled over salad greens.

Sesame seeds
These tiny white seeds are used in oriental cooking and lend a subtle savoury flavour and crunch to fried foods. They also provide an attractive nutty finish to breads and pastries.

Star anise
This pretty star-shaped spice is the fruit and seed pod of an evergreen tree. It is an important part of Chinese cooking, imparting a deep aniseed or liquorice flavour. Use in marinades and in duck and pork dishes.

fresh chillies

sesame seeds

dried root ginger

nutmeg

star anise

cinnamon

cayenne pepper

poppy seeds

cardamom pods

coriander seeds

dried mustard powder

chilli flakes

min

fennel seeds

hot red chillies

aniseed

peppercorns

mustard seeds

paprika

sea salt

garlic

Store Cupboard Nibbles

It is always a good idea to keep a variety of nuts and other nibbles in the cupboard. Often a few crisps, peanuts or olives are all you need to offer with drinks before going out or before a meal. Look in speciality shops and ethnic markets for unusual nibbles.

Bread sticks (grissini)
Stand these in a jug for an easy snack on their own or with something to dip into, or spread each with a little herb butter.

Bombay mix
Commercially prepared versions of this Indian snack are now widely available. A mixture of fried nuts, pulses and other nibbles flavoured with curry spices – perfect before an Indian meal.

Cheese straws
These cheese-flavoured twists of flaky pastry look pretty and make a tasty snack.

Dried apricots
Dried fruit makes an interesting alternative to the salty savoury nibble. Also, try dried peaches, dates, prunes, figs and banana chips for a healthy snack.

Dried cranberries
Dried cranberries are relatively new in the dried fruit selection of most supermarkets. They are good on their own or mixed with dried cherries.

Gherkins
Little sweet pickled gherkins are delicious as an appetizer as well as being low in calories.

Green olives
A wide variety of olives is available in supermarkets. For a party snack the stoned variety are the most convenient. Spanish olives are often stuffed with tiny pieces of red pimento, almonds or anchovies.

Honey roast cashews
These biscuity-flavoured nuts have a slightly sweet, honey coating.

Japanese rice crackers
These puffs of rice with peanuts inside or wrapped with dried seaweed make a sophisticated nibble and look very attractive.

Macadamia nuts
These nuts come from Hawaii and Australia and have a delicate sweetish flavour. They are expensive but delicious.

Pistachios
Always popular, but often expensive, these pretty green nuts are sold still in their shells. Don't forget to provide little dishes for the empty shells.

Pitta crisps
These triangles of pitta bread brushed with oil and sprinkled with herbs, and baked until crisp and golden, provide a crunchy snack.

Popcorn
Plain popcorn makes a healthy low-calorie snack. Tossed with butter or oil and salt, it is even more delicious, but more calorific. Various flavours of pre-popped corn can be found in most supermarkets.

Potato crisps
Universally popular, crisps come in a bewildering variety of flavours.

Prawn crackers
These commercially made pale puffs are crunchy and scented with prawn flavour. They are often served in Chinese or Thai restaurants.

Pretzel sticks
A delicious crunchy snack, these salty sticks are handy to keep as a stand-by, and easy to serve.

Tortilla chips
Triangles of fried corn, these little tortillas are ideal with a drink or cocktail like a margarita. They are also sold with chilli flavouring.

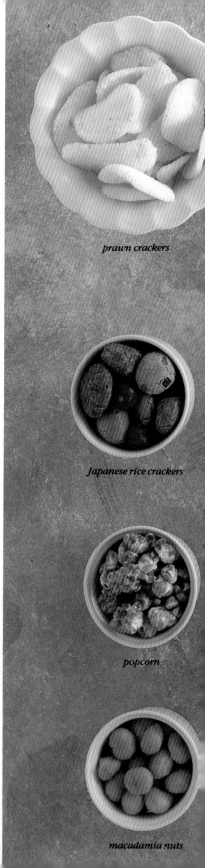

prawn crackers

Japanese rice crackers

popcorn

macadamia nuts

cheese straws

pitta crisps

tortilla chips

dried apricots

gherkins

green olives

Bombay mix

pistachios

potato crisps

dried cranberries

bread sticks (grissini)

pretzel sticks

honey roast cashews

Drinks

Without drinks there is no party, so you need to offer something even if it is only lemonade! No one expects your house to be a pub and a small party can probably be managed with a bottle or two of white wine in the fridge, maybe a red, and some soft drinks and bottled water.

Deciding what to serve and quantities can be tricky. Remember that spirits don't go off and most off-licenses supply on a sale or return policy, so it is best to over-estimate. You might choose to offer only wine or Champagne before a small dinner party; or you could set up a small bar, with one or two spirits such as gin or vodka and a sherry, as well as wine. For a bigger party, a bar with mixers for two or three cocktails could help set a theme. Your budget will probably be the deciding factor but, whatever you offer, always have lots of water, soft drinks and fruit juice for non-drinkers and children.

One bottle of wine will fill six average glasses, but if you are only serving wine or Champagne, allow half a bottle per person. Most people drink white wine at a drinks party, but plan on one-third drinking red. By far the easiest plan is to decide what you want to serve and offer a filled glass to your guests as they enter. Champagne is very festive and creates an instant party atmosphere. Almost nobody refuses it and there are lots of

other good bubbly substitutes on the market, such as Italian proseccos, Spanish Cavas and New World sparkling Chardonnays. Serve on its own or mixed with a little raspberry or blackcurrant liqueur (a kir), orange juice (Buck's Fizz) or peach juice (a Bellini); this will also give you more drinks per bottle.

If refrigerator space is at a premium, fill a bath tub, hand basin, large cooler or even a clean dustbin with lots of ice to cool the wine, water and soft drinks. Allow two glasses per person, as people tend to abandon their glasses as they move around. Wine shops often lend glasses if you buy a case of wine, or buy extras to keep on hand for parties. A standard white wine or tulip glass can be used for just about anything. If it is a large party, set up an extra wine station in another part of the room, with a few bottles on ice and some extra glasses; this helps prevent a bottle-neck at your primary bar or in the kitchen.

Remember, the most important thing is for you and your guests to relax and enjoy yourselves, so keep everything simple.

Garnishes

Garnishes on party food need to last longer than those on a dinner plate, which are eaten immediately – so keep them simple. Green, yellow and red tend to bring out the colour in foods, so stick to what looks best.

LEMON/CUCUMBER TWISTS

1 With a canelle knife, remove strips of peel down the length of the lemon or cucumber. Slice thinly then make a slit from one edge to the centre of each slice.

2 Twist the sides in opposite directions to form a twist.

RADISH FANS

1 Using a sharp knife, cut lengthways slits, leaving the stem end intact.

2 Gently push the radish to one side, causing the slices to fan out.

CHILLI FLOWERS

1 Slit the chillies lengthways and gently scrape out any seeds. Cut lengthways into as many strips as possible, leaving the stem ends intact.

2 Drop the chillies into a bowl of iced water and refrigerate several hours until curled. (The iced water causes the strips to curl back.)

SPRING ONION POMPOMS

1 Trim the spring onions and cut each into lengths of about 7.5 cm/3 in.

2 Using a small knife, cut as many slits lengthways as possible, leaving the root end intact. Drop into a bowl of iced water and refrigerate for several hours or overnight until curled. (The iced water causes the strips to curl back.)

Roasting Sweet Peppers

1 Place the peppers on a foil-lined baking sheet and grill until blackened and blistered on all sides, turning occasionally. Cover the peppers with a large bowl or place in a plastic bag and seal, until cool.

2 Using a sharp knife, peel off the charred skin. Cut the peppers into strips, removing the core and seeds but reserving any juices.

Lining Small Tartlet Tins

1 Roll out the dough as the recipe directs. Arrange the tartlet tins close to each other on a work surface. Roll the dough loosely back on to the rolling pin then roll out over the tins. Roll the rolling pin firmly over the dough to cut the edges.

2 Using both thumbs, carefully press the dough into the bottom and up the sides of the tins.

Using a Canelle Knife

1 Holding the fruit or vegetable in one hand, pull the canelle knife along the surface at regular intervals to create grooves in the surface.

2 Cut the fruit or vegetable horizontally to make pretty, ridged slices.

Easy Sauces and Spreads

MAYONNAISE

Home-made mayonnaise is well worth making to use as a spread or dip. If you like, add some herbs along with the egg yolks. Remember mayonnaise is made with raw egg yolks, so use fresh eggs from a good supplier. Raw eggs are not suitable for young children, the elderly or pregnant women.

Makes about 350 ml/12 fl oz/1½ cups

INGREDIENTS
2 egg yolks
15 ml/1 tbsp Dijon mustard
15 ml/1 tbsp white wine vinegar
300 ml/½ pint/1¼ cups olive oil or
    half olive oil and half sunflower oil

1 Put the egg yolks in the bowl of a food processor. Add the mustard and vinegar and process for 10 seconds to blend.

2 With the machine running, gradually pour the oil through the feed tube in a steady stream until all the oil is incorporated and the sauce is thickened. Add 15–30 ml/1–2 tbsp boiling water and process briefly to blend. Will keep in the fridge for up to 2 or 3 days.

EASY PESTO SAUCE

Pesto is a delicious sauce which can be used on its own or stirred into sour cream or mayonnaise to use as a quick dip. Use a good quality olive oil.

Makes about 300 ml/½ pint/1¼ cups

INGREDIENTS
50 g/2 oz/about 2 cups fresh basil
    leaves
1–2 garlic cloves
45 ml/3 tbsp freshly grated Parmesan
    cheese
45 ml/3 tbsp pine nuts, lightly toasted
salt
freshly ground black pepper
60–90 ml/4–6 tbsp virgin olive oil,
    plus extra for sealing

1 Put the basil leaves, garlic, Parmesan cheese and pine nuts in the bowl of a food processor. Season with salt and pepper and process until well blended, scraping down the side of the bowl once or twice.

2 With the machine running, gradually pour the oil through the feed tube until a smooth paste forms. Pour into a jar and spoon over a little more oil to seal the surface. Cover tightly and refrigerate, where it will keep for up to one week, or freeze in smaller quantities.

QUICK TAPENADE

Tapenade is an olive spread used in the Mediterranean as a tasty snack spread on toasts, or stirred into soups and stews. Keep it on hand for quick *crostini* or stir into soft cheese for an easy spread or dip.

Makes about 250 ml/8 fl oz/1 cup

INGREDIENTS
100 g/4 oz/⅔ cup Kalamata, or other
   oil-cured black olives, stoned
1–2 garlic cloves, chopped
15 ml/1 tbsp capers, rinsed

45 ml/3 tbsp virgin olive oil, plus
   extra for sealing
2–4 anchovy fillets, drained
juice of ½ lemon
5–10 ml/1–2 tsp chopped fresh

1 Put all the ingredients except the coriander into the bowl of a food processor and process until finely chopped, scraping down the side of the bowl once or twice.

2 Spoon into a small bowl and stir in the chopped coriander. Spoon over a little extra olive oil to seal. Cover and refrigerate up to two weeks.

BASIC TOMATO SAUCE

This sauce can be used as the base for pasta or vegetable sauces, as a pizza base or a seasoned dip. Use ripe tomatoes with lots of flavour and your favourite herbs.

Makes about 325 ml/11 fl oz/1⅓ cups

INGREDIENTS
30 ml/2 tbsp olive oil
1 large onion, chopped
1–2 garlic cloves, chopped
2.5 ml/½ tsp chopped fresh thyme
   leaves or 1.25 ml/¼ tsp dried
   thyme
1–2 bay leaves
6–8 ripe plum tomatoes
50 ml/2 fl oz/¼ cup water or stock
5–10 ml/1–2 tsp chopped fresh herbs

1 In a large frying pan or saucepan heat the olive oil over a medium heat. Add the onions and cook for 5–7 minutes, stirring frequently until softened. Add the garlic, thyme and bay leaves and cook for 1 minute longer. Stir in the tomatoes and water or stock. Bring to the boil and cook, uncovered, for 15–20 minutes over a medium heat until most of the liquid has evaporated and the sauce has thickened.

2 Pour into the bowl of a food processor and process until smooth. Strain through a sieve to remove any skin and pips, then stir in the herbs. Cool and refrigerate, keeps for up to four days.

Hot Pepper Pecans

These nuts are easy to make and can be prepared up to a week ahead, then stored in an airtight container.

Makes about 350 g/12 oz/3 cups

INGREDIENTS
15 g/½ oz/1 tbsp butter
15 ml/1 tbsp sesame oil
350 g/12 oz/3 cups pecan halves
15–30 ml/1–2 tbsp soy sauce
2–3 dashes hot pepper sauce, or
   to taste
15 ml/1 tbsp clear honey (optional)

pecan halves

sesame oil

soy sauce

honey

pepper sauce

butter

1 Preheat the oven to 150°C/300°F/ Gas 2. Put the butter and oil on a medium-sized baking sheet and heat in the oven until the butter melts. Remove and swirl to blend. Stir in the pecans until well coated, then toast in the oven for 30 minutes stirring once or twice.

2 Sprinkle the soy sauce over the nuts, then add a few dashes of hot pepper sauce and the honey, if using. Toss the nuts until well coated, then allow to cool. Store in an airtight container.

Easy Nachos

This Tex-Mex speciality is popular throughout the USA, a spicy cheese snack that can be made in minutes.

Makes 24

INGREDIENTS
2–3 fresh or pickled jalapeño or other
   medium-hot chilli peppers
24 large tortilla chips
175 g/6 oz/scant 2 cups grated
   Cheddar cheese
2 spring onions, finely chopped
sour cream, to serve (optional)

chilli peppers

tortilla chips

sour cream

grated Cheddar cheese

spring onions

COOK'S TIP
When handling chillies, wear rubber gloves and be sure to wash your knife and cutting board well, as the chilli oils can irritate skin and eyes.

1 With a small sharp knife, split the chilli peppers and remove the seeds (the hottest part). Slice thinly.

2 Preheat the oven to 220°C/425°F/ Gas 7. Arrange the tortilla chips in a single layer on a large baking sheet lined with foil. Sprinkle a little grated cheese on to each tortilla chip and top with a slice of chilli and a few spring onions. Bake for about 5 minutes until golden and bubbling. Serve hot with sour cream, if you like.

Spicy Microwave Poppadums

This is a wonderfully easy way to prepare a spicy snack. Poppadums are traditionally fried, but this method is much lighter.

Makes 6 or 12

INGREDIENTS
6 poppadums, broken in half if you wish
vegetable oil, for brushing
cayenne pepper or chilli powder

poppadums

vegetable oil

chilli powder

1 Lay the poppadums on a work surface and brush each one lightly with a little vegetable oil. Sprinkle with a pinch of cayenne pepper or chilli powder.

2 Arrange 2–4 poppadums (depending on the size of your microwave) on paper towels and microwave on High (100%) for 40–60 seconds. Serve immediately.

VARIATION

If you don't have a microwave you can make the same snack by using poppadums which can be grilled, and following the instructions on the packet after step one.

Hot and Spicy Popcorn

This is an ideal nibble for a crowd. Making your own popcorn is easy, but you can use the ready-made, shop-bought variety if you like. Adjust the chilli powder to suit your taste.

Makes 175 g/6 oz/12 cups

INGREDIENTS
120 ml/4 fl oz/½ cup vegetable oil, plus extra for popping
175 g/6 oz/1 cup unpopped popcorn
2–3 garlic cloves, crushed
5–10 ml/1–2 tsp chilli powder (according to taste)
pinch cayenne pepper
salt

vegetable oil

popcorn

garlic cloves

cayenne pepper

chilli powder

1 In a large heavy saucepan, heat the extra oil, then pop the corn according to the manufacturer's instructions.

2 In a small saucepan, combine the oil, the garlic cloves, chilli powder and cayenne pepper. Cook over low heat for about 5 minutes, stirring occasionally. Remove the garlic cloves with a slotted spoon, then pour the flavoured oil over the popcorn. Toss well to combine and season with salt to taste. Serve warm or at room temperature.

VARIATION

For Parmesan Popcorn omit the chilli powder and salt and proceed as above. After pouring over the seasoned oil, add 60–90 ml/4–6 tbsp freshly grated Parmesan cheese, and toss well.

Celery Sticks with Roquefort

This delicious filling can also be made with English Stilton or any other blue cheese. Diluted with a little milk or cream, it also makes a delicious dip.

Makes about 45

INGREDIENTS
7 ounces Roquefort or other blue
   cheese, softened
1¼ cups lowfat cream cheese
2 green onions, finely chopped
black pepper
1 to 2 tablespoons milk
1 celery head
chopped walnuts or hazelnuts, to
   garnish

green onions

*lowfat
cream cheese*

*Roquefort
cheese*

*chopped
walnuts*

celery

1 With a fork, crumble the Roquefort in a bowl. Put in a food processor with the cream cheese, green onions, and black pepper. Process until smooth, scraping down the side of the bowl once or twice and gradually adding milk if the mixture seems too stiff.

2 If you like, peel the celery lightly to remove any heavy strings before cutting each stalk into 3- to 4-inch pieces. Using a small knife, fill each celery stick with a little cheese mixture and press on a few chopped nuts. Arrange on a serving plate and refrigerate until ready to serve.

COOK'S TIP

For a more elegant presentation, fill a pastry bag fitted with a small star tip with the cheese mixture and carefully pipe mixture into the celery sticks. Press on the nuts.

Italian-style Marinated Artichokes

Good-quality extra-virgin olive oil together with fresh herbs, turn canned or frozen artichoke hearts into a delicious snack.

Makes about 750 ml/1¼ pints/3 cups

INGREDIENTS
2 × 14-ounce cans artichoke hearts
   in salt water
¾ cup extra-virgin olive oil
1 teaspoon chopped fresh thyme, or
   ½ teaspoon dried thyme
1 teaspoon chopped fresh oregano or
   marjoram, or ½ teaspoon dried
   oregano or marjoram
½ teaspoon fennel seeds, lightly
   crushed
1 to 2 garlic cloves, finely chopped
freshly ground black pepper
grated peel and juice of ½ lemon

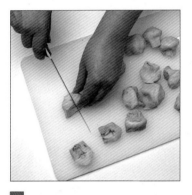

1 Rinse the artichokes, then drain them on paper towels. Cut any large ones in half lengthwise.

thyme

*artichoke
hearts*

lemon

black pepper

oregano

lemon zest

*extra-virgin
olive oil*

fennel seeds

2 Put the artichokes in a large saucepan with the next six ingredients, stir to combine, then cook, covered, over very low heat for 8 to 10 minutes until the flavors infuse. Remove from the heat and leave to cool slightly, then gently stir in the lemon peel and juice. Refrigerate. Return to room temperature before serving on toothpicks.

Parma-Wrapped Grissini

This is an easy way to combine two well-loved ingredients for a quick nibble with no real cooking.

Makes about 24

INGREDIENTS
225 g/8 oz Parma ham, very thinly
    sliced
1 × 115 g/4 oz box grissini (Italian
    bread sticks)
basil leaves, to garnish (optional)

grissini

basil leaves

Parma ham

1 If the Parma ham slices are large, lay each slice flat on a board and cut in half lengthways.

2 Wrap each bread stick with a half-slice of Parma ham, tucking in a basil leaf if you like, to come half way down the bread stick. Arrange on a plate and cover until ready to serve. Garnish with fresh basil if you like.

COOK'S TIP
Do not prepare too far in advance as the moisture from the ham will cause the bread sticks to bend.

VARIATION
Substitute half-slices of thinly smoked salmon and garnish with sprigs of dill instead of basil.

Aromatic Greek Olives with Feta

Prepare lots of these and store them in the refrigerator for unexpected guests. They will keep for about a month in a tightly closed container, but remember to bring them to room temperature before serving.

Makes 450 g/1 lb/3 cups

INGREDIENTS
175 ml/6 fl oz/¾ cup virgin olive oil
15 ml/1 tbsp cumin seeds, lightly
    crushed
15 ml/1 tbsp coriander seeds, lightly
    crushed
15 ml/1 tbsp fennel seeds, lightly
    crushed
5 ml/1 tsp cardamom pods, crushed
2.5 ml/½ tsp crushed red pepper
    flakes
1.25 ml/¼ tsp ground cinnamon
4–6 garlic cloves, crushed
grated zest and juice of 1 lemon
450 g/1 lb/3 cups Kalamata or other
    oil-cured olives, drained

TO SERVE
225 g/8 oz feta cheese, cut into
    1 cm/½ in cubes
15–30 ml/1–2 tbsp virgin olive oil
freshly ground black pepper
15–30 ml/1–2 tbsp chopped fresh
    parsley or coriander

feta cheese   *Kalamata olives*

lemon

olive oil

lemon zest

coriander

coriander seeds

cardamom pods

garlic cloves

red pepper flakes

cinnamon

fennel seeds

1 In a medium-sized saucepan, combine the olive oil, spices and garlic. Cook over medium-low heat for 3–5 minutes until warm and fragrant, stirring occasionally.

COOK'S TIP
The seasoned feta cheese cubes make a delicious nibble on their own.

2 Remove the pan from the heat and stir in the lemon zest and juice, then add the olives, tossing until well combined. Set aside to cool. Transfer to an airtight container or jar to refrigerate.

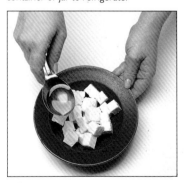

3 Bring the olives to room temperature, and pour into a bowl. Put the feta cubes in another bowl, drizzle over the olive oil, season with black pepper, then sprinkle with chopped parsley or coriander. Serve the olives with the cheese cubes.

Parmesan Filo Triangles

You can whip up these light and crunchy triangles at the last minute using fresh or frozen sheets of filo pastry.

Makes about 24

INGREDIENTS
3 large sheets filo pastry
olive oil, for brushing
45–60 ml/3–4 tbsp freshly grated
   Parmesan cheese
2.5 ml/½ tsp crumbled dried thyme
   or sage

Parmesan cheese

olive oil

filo pastry

1 Preheat the oven to 180°C/350°F/ Gas 4. Line a large baking sheet with foil and brush lightly with oil. Lay one sheet of filo pastry on a work surface and brush lightly with a little olive oil. Sprinkle lightly with half the Parmesan and a little dried thyme or sage. Cover with a second sheet of filo, brush with a little more oil and sprinkle with the remaining cheese and thyme or sage. Top with the remaining sheets of filo and brush very lightly with a little more oil.

2 With a sharp knife, cut the filo pastry stack in half lengthways and then into squares. Cut each square into triangles.

3 Arrange the triangles on the baking sheet, scrunching them slightly. Do not allow them to touch. Bake for 6–8 minutes until crisp and golden. Cool slightly and serve immediately.

COOK'S TIP

These will keep in an airtight container for up to three days, but handle carefully as they are very fragile. Reheat in a moderate oven to crisp when you are ready to serve them.

Mini Macaroons

Try these chewy macaroons with a glass of wine – in France, sweet biscuits are often served with Champagne.

Makes about 34

INGREDIENTS
150 g/5 oz/1¼ cups blanched almonds
150 g/5 oz/⅔ cup + 15 ml/1 tbsp caster sugar
2 egg whites
2.5 ml/½ tsp almond or natural vanilla essence
icing sugar, for dusting (optional)

egg white

caster sugar

almond essence

blanched almonds

1 Preheat the oven to 200°C/400°F/Gas 6. Line a large baking sheet with non-stick baking parchment. Put the almonds and sugar in the bowl of a food processor and process until very finely ground. With the machine running, slowly add the egg whites. (You may not need all of them; the dough should be soft but hold its shape.) If the mixture is too stiff, add a little more egg white. Carefully mix in the almond or vanilla essence.

2 With moistened hands, shape the mixture into about 34 small balls and arrange on the baking sheet about 4 cm/1½ in apart. With the back of a wet spoon, flatten the tops and dust lightly with icing sugar.

3 Bake for 12–15 minutes until the tops just begin to colour and the macaroons feel slightly firm. Transfer the baking sheet to a wire rack to cool, dust with more icing sugar if you like, then remove the macaroons from the paper.

VARIATION

If you like, press an extra blanched almond half on top of each macaroon before baking.

Crudités and Dips

Dips and their accompanying raw vegetables – crudités – seem to be an inevitable feature of any informal gathering, because they are such ideal party food. Just about anything can be included in the crudité category – asparagus spears, courgettes, raw or blanched vegetables, strips of cheese, melon, cooked chicken . . . all these can be dipped into a variety of mixtures that come from around the world – guacamole from Mexico, hummus and taramasalata from Greece, sweet mustard sauce from Sweden, spicy dhal from India, olivada from Spain or tapenade from France. The following two dips are easy to make and can be prepared at the last minute.

Slicing Peppers

 Cut off the bottom of the pepper and stand the pepper on the cut edge. Cut down each side of the core to obtain 4 flat sides.

2 Cut each side into triangular-shaped spears to serve as crudités.

Easy Oriental Dip

Makes about 250 ml/ 8 fl oz/1 cup

INGREDIENTS
120 ml/4 fl oz/½ cup sunflower oil
50 ml/2 fl oz/¼ cup toasted sesame oil
2.5 cm/1 in piece fresh root ginger, peeled
1–2 garlic cloves, crushed
2 spring onions, finely chopped
1 small red chilli, seeds removed, finely chopped

sesame oil

spring onions

soy sauce

root ginger *garlic* *sunflower oil*

I Heat the oils in a small saucepan over a low heat. Cut the peeled root ginger into thin slices. Stack the slices and cut into long thin julienne strips.

2 Turn the strips and cut crossways into very small dice. Put the diced ginger, garlic, spring onions and chilli into the oil and heat for 5–7 minutes, to allow the flavours to infuse. Cool and pour into a small bowl and serve with crudités.

VARIATION

Try making a sour cream and herb dip by mixing together 250 ml/8 oz/1 cup sour cream, 2 spring onions finely chopped, and sprigs of fresh herbs such as dill, parsley and chives. Season with black pepper, you can also add crushed garlic to this dip.

Slicing Fennel

1 Trim the tops and root end of the fennel bulb. If you like, remove the triangular core and cut the bulb in half lengthways.

2 Cut each half into long strips to serve as crudités.

Tortelloni Kebabs

This hors d'oeuvres is easy to make, and always popular. Any favourite dipping sauce can be substituted, or just drizzle the kebabs with good virgin olive oil and sprinkle with freshly grated Parmesan.

Makes about 64

INGREDIENTS
450 g/1 lb fresh cheese-filled
   tortelloni
10 ml/2 tsp olive oil
basil leaves, to garnish

FOR THE SAUCE
1 × 450 g/16 oz jar roasted red
   peppers, drained
1 garlic clove, chopped
15 ml/1 tbsp olive oil
15 ml/1 tbsp balsamic vinegar
5 ml/1 tsp sugar
freshly ground black pepper
2–3 dashes hot pepper sauce

garlic

roasted
red pepper

olive oil

tortelloni

hot pepper sauce

basil

sugar

balsamic
vinegar

1 Put the ingredients for the sauce into the bowl of a food processor and process until smooth, scraping down the sides once or twice. Sieve into a serving bowl and cover until ready to serve.

2 Bring a large saucepan of lightly salted water to a fast boil. Add the tortelloni and cook according to the instructions on the packet, for 8–10 minutes. Drain, rinse in warm water and turn into a bowl. Toss with olive oil to prevent sticking. Cover until ready to serve.

3 Using small, 15 cm/6 in wooden skewers, thread a basil leaf and 1 tortelloni on to each skewer. Arrange on a plate and serve warm, or at room temperature with the dipping sauce.

COOK'S TIP
The sauce can be made up to a day in advance or frozen for several weeks.

Hot Salt Beef on a Stick

This quick nibble on a stick is based on the famous New York delicatessen sandwich, pastrami on rye.

Makes 24

INGREDIENTS
vegetable oil, for frying
unsliced rye bread with caraway
    seeds, cut into 24 1 cm/½ in cubes
225 g/8 oz salt beef or pastrami, in one
    piece
mild mustard, for spreading
2 pickled cucumbers, cut into
    small pieces
24 cocktail onions

salt beef

rye bread

mustard

cocktail onions

pickled cucumbers

1 In a heavy medium-sized frying pan, heat 1 cm/½ in of oil. When very hot but not smoking add half the bread cubes and fry for about 1 minute until just golden, turning occasionally. Remove with a slotted spoon and drain on a paper towel. Repeat with the remaining cubes.

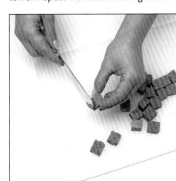

2 Cut the salt beef or pastrami into 1 cm/½ in cubes and spread one side of each cube with a little mustard.

3 Thread a bread cube on to a skewer then a piece of meat with the mustard side against the bread, then a piece of pickled cucumber, and finally an onion. Arrange the skewers on a plate or tray, and serve immediately.

Medjoul Dates Stuffed with Cream Cheese

These soft, plump fresh dates make an ideal snack. They are now available in most large supermarkets.

Makes 24

INGREDIENTS
24 fresh medjoul dates
225 g/8 oz cream cheese, softened
zest and juice of ½ orange
15–30 ml/1–2 tbsp Amaretto liqueur
  (optional)
50 g/2 oz/½ cup toasted almonds,
  coarsely chopped

orange

tortelloni

medjoul dates

toasted almonds

cream cheese

1 With a small sharp knife, split each date lengthways and remove the stone. In a small bowl, beat the cream cheese with the orange zest and 30–45 ml/2–3 tbsp of the juice. Stir in the Amaretto if using.

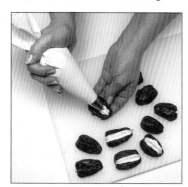

2 Spoon the mixture into a small piping bag fitted with a medium star or plain nozzle. Pipe a line of filling into each date, then sprinkle with the nuts.

VARIATION
You can use small dates but they are stickier and more fiddly to prepare.

Hot Crab Dip

This delicious creamy dip with a golden almond crust is served hot, with raw vegetables or savoury biscuits.

Makes about 600 ml/1 pint/2½ cups

INGREDIENTS
225 g/8 oz cream cheese, at room
  temperature
30–45 ml/2–3 tbsp milk
15 ml/1 tbsp Cognac or vermouth
2 spring onions, finely chopped
5–10 ml/1–2 tsp Dijon mustard
salt
2–3 dashes hot pepper sauce
15 ml/1 tbsp chopped fresh dill or
  parsley
225 g/8 oz white crab meat, picked
  over
45–60 ml/3–4 tbsp flaked almonds

crab meat

spring onions

cream cheese

Dijon mustard

dill

hot pepper sauce

vermouth

flaked almonds

1 Preheat the oven to 190°C/375°F/ Gas 5. In a bowl, beat the cream cheese with all the other ingredients except the almonds.

2 Spoon the mixture into a small gratin or baking dish and sprinkle with the almonds. Bake for 12–15 minutes until the top is golden and the crab mixture hot and bubbling. Serve immediately with a selection of raw vegetables or savoury biscuits.

Mini Jacket Potatoes with Sour Cream and Chives

Jacket potatoes are always delicious, and the toppings can easily be varied – from caviar and smoked salmon to cheese and baked beans.

Makes 36

INGREDIENTS
36 potatoes, about 4 cm/1½ in
    in diameter, well scrubbed
250 ml/8 fl oz/1 cup thick sour cream
45–60 ml/3–4 tbsp snipped fresh
    chives
coarse salt, for sprinkling

sour cream

potatoes

chives

1 Preheat the oven to 180°C/350°F/ Gas 4. Place potatoes on a baking sheet and bake for 30–35 minutes, or until tender when pierced with the tip of a knife.

2 To serve, make a cross in the top of each potato and squeeze gently to open. Using the handle of a wooden spoon, make a hole in the centre of each potato. Fill each hole with a little sour cream, then sprinkle with the salt and the chives. Serve immediately, or at room temperature.

VARIATION
If your guests are likely to be hungry, use medium size potatoes. When cooked, cut in half, scoop out the flesh, mash with the other ingredients and spoon the mixture back into the skin. Serve warm.

COOK'S TIP
The potatoes can be baked in advance, then reheated in the microwave on High (100%) for 3–4 minutes.

36

Savoury Cheese Balls

These colourful little cheese balls are made in four different flavours, each variety coated with a different herb or seed.

Makes about 48

INGREDIENTS

450 g/1 lb/2⅔ cups cream cheese at room temperature
25 g/1 oz/¼ cup grated mature Cheddar cheese
2.5 ml/½ tsp dry mustard powder, prepared
5 ml/1 tsp mango chutney, chopped (optional)
cayenne pepper
salt
50 g/2 oz Roquefort or Stilton cheese
15 ml/1 tbsp finely chopped spring onions or snipped fresh chives
5–10 ml/1–2 tsp bottled pesto sauce
15 ml/1 tbsp chopped pine nuts
1–2 garlic cloves, finely chopped
30 ml/2 tbsp chopped mixed fresh herbs, such as parsley, tarragon, chives, dill or coriander

TO COAT

30 ml/2 tbsp paprika
30 ml/2 tbsp finely chopped fresh parsley
30 ml/2 tbsp toasted sesame seeds
coarsely ground black pepper mixed with poppy seeds

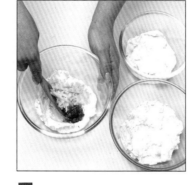

1 Divide the cream cheese equally among four small bowls. Into one mix the Cheddar cheese, mustard and mango chutney if using. Season with cayenne pepper and a little salt. Into the second bowl, mix the Roquefort or Stilton cheese and spring onions or chives and season with a little cayenne.

2 Mix the pesto sauce and pine nuts into the third bowl and season with a little cayenne. Mix the chopped garlic and mixed fresh herbs into the last bowl of cream cheese. Cover and refrigerate all four bowls for about 30 minutes, until the cheese is firm enough to handle. Roll each of the different cheese mixtures into small balls, keeping them separate.

3 Lightly dust the Cheddar flavoured balls with paprika, rolling to cover completely. Roll the pesto balls in chopped parsley and the Roquefort balls in sesame seeds. Roll the garlic-herb cheese balls in coarsely ground black pepper and poppy seeds. Arrange the balls on leaves, a plate or in a lined basket and serve with cocktail sticks.

spring onions
sesame seeds
garlic
parsley
Cheddar cheese
cream cheese
poppy seeds
pesto sauce
Roquefort cheese
black pepper
dry mustard
paprika
cayenne pepper
chopped pine nuts
mango chutney

Crostini with Three Vegetable Toppings

This popular Italian hors d'oeuvre was originally a way of using up leftovers such as ham, cheese and pâté.

Makes 24

INGREDIENTS
1 ciabatta or French stick

FOR THE ONION AND BLACK OLIVE TOPPING
15 ml/1 tbsp olive oil
2 red onions, thinly sliced
5 ml/1 tsp sugar
2.5 ml/½ tsp dried thyme
16 Kalamata or other oil-cured black olives, stoned and halved
bottled tapenade, for spreading (optional)
parsley leaves, to garnish

FOR THE PEPPER AND ANCHOVY TOPPING
1 × 400 g/14 oz jar Italian roasted red peppers
50 g/2 oz can anchovy fillets
extra-virgin olive oil, for drizzling
15–30 ml/1–2 tbsp balsamic vinegar
1 garlic clove, peeled
30 ml/2 tbsp chopped fresh chives, oregano or sage, to garnish
15 ml/1 tbsp capers, to garnish

FOR THE MOZZARELLA AND TOMATO TOPPING
pesto sauce, for brushing
120 ml/4 fl oz/½ cup thick home-made or bottled tomato sauce or pizza topping
115 g/4 oz good quality mozzarella cheese, cut into 8 thin slices
2–3 ripe plum tomatoes, seeded and cut into strips
fresh basil leaves, to garnish

ciabatta

tapenade

red onions

Kalamata olives

olive oil

tomato sauce

basil

plum tomatoes

mozzarella cheese

anchovy fillets

balsamic vinegar

chives

capers

garlic

roasted red peppers

1 Cut the ciabatta or French bread into 24 slices, 1 cm/½ in thick. Toast until crisp and golden on both sides. Cool on a wire rack.

2 Prepare the Onion and Black Olive Topping, in a heavy medium frying pan. Heat the olive oil over medium heat and add the onions. Cook slowly for 7–10 minutes, stirring frequently until soft and just beginning to colour. Stir in the sugar, thyme and olives and remove from the heat to cool. Spread 8 of the toasts with a little tapenade and top with a generous spoonful of the onion mixture. Garnish with parsley.

3 For the Pepper and Anchovy Topping, drain the peppers and wipe dry. Cut into 1 cm/½ in strips and place in a shallow dish. Rinse and dry the anchovy fillets and add to the peppers. Drizzle with olive oil and sprinkle with the vinegar. Rub 8 toasts with the garlic clove. Arrange the peppers and anchovies on the toasts and sprinkle with herbs and capers. For the Mozzarella and Tomato Topping, brush the remaining 8 toasts with pesto sauce and spoon tomato sauce onto each. Arrange a slice of mozzarella cheese on each and cover with the tomato strips. Garnish with basil.

Grilled Brie with Walnuts

This unusual cheese snack looks impressive but requires almost no preparation.

Serves about 16–20

INGREDIENTS
15 g/½ oz/1 tbsp butter, at room
  temperature
5 ml/1 tsp Dijon mustard
675 g/1½ lb wheel of Brie or
  Camembert cheese
25 g/1 oz/¼ cup chopped walnuts
French stick, sliced and toasted,
  to serve

Dijon mustard

Brie wheel

walnuts

butter

1 Preheat the grill. In a small bowl, cream together the butter and mustard, and spread evenly over the surface of the cheese. Transfer to a flameproof serving plate and grill 4–6 inches from the heat, for 3–4 minutes until the top just begins to bubble.

2 Sprinkle the surface with the walnuts and grill for 2–3 minutes longer until the nuts are golden. Serve immediately with the French bread toasts. Allow your guests to help themselves as the whole brie makes an attractive centrepiece.

Spicy Oven-baked Potato Boats

These tasty spiced potato wedges are easy to make, and disappear so quickly it's a good idea to double the recipe!

Makes about 38 wedges

INGREDIENTS
4 medium-sized waxy potatoes, such
  as Desirée, scrubbed and unpeeled
1 garlic clove, crushed
15 ml/1 tbsp cumin seeds
2.5 ml/½ tsp ground coriander
2.5 ml/½ tsp ground black pepper
90 ml/3 fl oz/⅓ cup virgin olive oil
salt

garlic

coriander

potatoes

olive oil

black pepper

cumin seed

1 Preheat the oven to 200°C/400°F/ Gas 6. Cut the potatoes into boat-shaped wedges about 2 cm/¾ in thick. Place in a large bowl and sprinkle with the garlic, cumin seeds, coriander, black pepper and olive oil and toss to coat well.

2 Lightly grease a large baking sheet (preferably non-stick) and warm in the oven. Then arrange the potatoes on the baking sheet in a single layer. Bake for 30–35 minutes until tender and golden brown. Sprinkle with salt and serve hot.

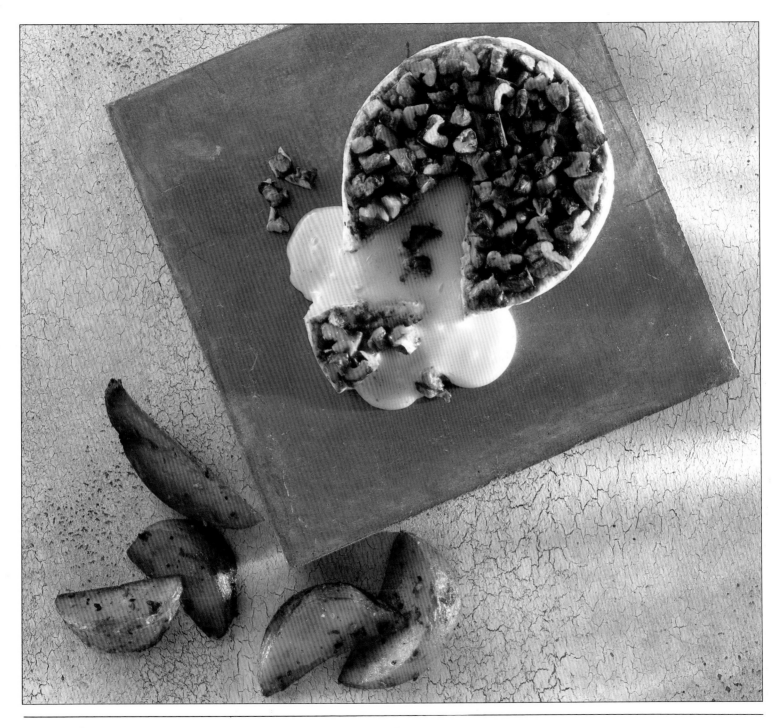

Tiny Cheese Puffs

These bite-sized portions of choux pastry are the ideal accompaniment to a glass of wine.

Makes about 45

INGREDIENTS
115 g/4 oz/1 cup plain flour
2.5 ml/½ tsp salt
5 ml/1 tsp dry mustard powder
pinch of cayenne pepper
250 ml/8 fl oz/1 cup water
125 g/4 oz/½ cup butter, cut into
    pieces
4 eggs
75 g/3 oz Gruyère cheese, finely diced
1 tbsp chives, finely chopped

plain flour

eggs

butter

cayenne pepper

Gruyère cheese

mustard powder

1 Preheat the oven to 200°C/400°F/ Gas 6. Lightly grease 2 large baking sheets. Sift together the flour, salt, dry mustard and cayenne pepper.

2 In a medium-sized saucepan, bring the water and butter to the boil over medium-high heat. Remove from the heat and add the flour mixture all at once, beating with a wooden spoon until the dough forms a ball. Return to the heat and beat constantly for 1–2 minutes to dry out. Remove from the heat and cool for 3–5 minutes.

3 Beat 3 of the eggs in to the dough, one at a time, beating well after each addition. Beat the fourth egg in a small bowl and add a teaspoon at a time beating until the dough is smooth and shiny and falls slowly when dropped from a spoon. (You may not need the all the fourth egg; reserve any remaining egg for glazing.) Stir in the diced cheese and chives.

4 Using 2 teaspoons, drop small mounds of dough 5 cm/2 in apart on to the baking sheets. Beat the reserved egg with 15 ml/1 tbsp water and brush the tops with the glaze. Bake for 8 minutes, then reduce the oven temperature to 180°C/ 350°F/Gas 4 and bake for 7–8 minutes more, until puffed and golden. Remove to a wire rack to cool. Serve warm.

VARIATION

For Ham and Cheese Puffs, add 50 g/ 2 oz finely diced ham with the cheese. For Cheesy Herb Puffs, stir in 30 ml/ 2 tbsp chopped fresh herbs or spring onions with the cheese.

COOK'S TIP

The puffs can be prepared ahead and even frozen. Reheat in a hot oven for 5 minutes, until crisp, before serving.

Straw Potato Cakes with Caramelized Apple

These little potato cakes resemble *latkes*, a Central European speciality. You must work quickly, as the potato darkens very rapidly.

Makes about 16

INGREDIENTS
15 g/½ oz/1 tbsp butter
1–2 dessert apples, unpeeled cored and diced
5 ml/1 tsp lemon juice
10 ml/2 tsp sugar
pinch cinnamon
55 ml/2 oz/¼ cup thick sour cream

FOR THE POTATO CAKES
½ small onion, very finely chopped or grated
2 medium-sized baking potatoes
salt
freshly ground black pepper
oil, for frying
flat-leaf parsley, to garnish

COOK'S TIP
Potato cakes can be prepared in advance and warmed in a preheated 200°C/400°F/Gas 6 oven for about 5–7 minutes, until heated through.

VARIATION
Omit the caramelized apple and top each cake with a few slices of smoked salmon, sprinkled with snipped chives.

1 In a medium-sized frying pan, melt the butter over medium heat. Add the diced apple and toss to coat. Sprinkle with the lemon juice, sugar and cinnamon and cook for 2–3 minutes, stirring frequently, until the apples are just tender and beginning to colour. Turn into a bowl.

2 Put the grated onion into a bowl. Using a hand or box grater, grate the potatoes on to a clean tea towel and squeeze the potato as dry as possible.

3 Shake into the bowl with the onion and season with the salt and pepper.

potatoes

onion

lemon

dessert apples

sugar

cinnamon

oil

butter

black pepper

4 In a large heavy frying pan heat 1 cm/½ in oil, until hot but not smoking. Drop tablespoonfuls of the potato mixture into the oil in batches.

5 Flatten slightly and cook for 5–6 minutes. Drain on paper towels. Keep warm. To serve, top each potato cake with 5 ml/1 tsp caramelized apple and then a little sour cream on top. Garnish with flat-leaf parsley.

Angels and Devils on Horseback

The combination of bacon with scallops and chicken livers is surprisingly good. Prepare these in advance, then cook them at the last minute.

Makes 24

INGREDIENTS
12 rashers streaky bacon, rind
    removed
12 medium scallops, muscle
    extracted, rinsed and dried
salt and freshly ground black pepper
paprika
15–30 ml/1–2 tbsp chopped fresh
    parsley
12 small chicken livers, gristle and fat
    removed, dried on paper towels

streaky bacon

chicken liver

parsley

paprika

scallop

black pepper

1 Preheat the oven to 230°C/450°F/Gas 8. Line a large baking sheet with foil. Cut the bacon slices in half crossways and lay them on a work surface. Run the back of a large knife blade firmly along each rasher to flatten and stretch the bacon.

2 Place a scallop on each rasher and season with salt, pepper and paprika. Sprinkle with a little parsley. Place a chicken liver on the remaining rashers and season. Roll the scallops and livers up in the bacon and secure with a cocktail stick.

3 Arrange the bacon rolls on the baking sheet and cook for 8–10 minutes until the bacon is crisp and brown and the scallops and livers are just firm to the touch. Serve warm or at room temperature.

VARIATION

Fresh dates stuffed with almonds can be used instead of chicken livers.

Guacamole-filled Cherry Tomatoes

Cherry tomatoes are just the right size for an easy nibble; look for the yellow tomatoes in season. You can make the filling as mild or as spicy as you like.

Makes 24

INGREDIENTS
24 cherry tomatoes
salt
1 large ripe avocado, halved and stone removed
50 g/2 oz/⅓ cup cream cheese
3–4 dashes hot pepper sauce, or to taste
grated zest and juice of half a lime
15–30 ml/1–2 tbsp chopped fresh coriander

avocado

lime

pepper sauce

cream cheese

cherry tomatoes

coriander

1 Turn the tomatoes on to their sides on the chopping board. With a small sharp knife, cut a slice from the bottom of each tomato. Using the handle of a small spoon, scoop out the seeds and sprinkle the cavities with salt. Turn the tomatoes over and drain on paper towels for at least 30 minutes.

2 Scoop out the flesh of the avocado into the bowl of a food processor and add the cream cheese. Process until very smooth, scraping down the sides of the bowl once or twice. Season with salt, hot pepper sauce and the lime zest and juice. Add half the chopped coriander and process to blend.

COOK'S TIP

The tomatoes can be prepared the day before and stored, covered, in the refrigerator, ready for filling.

3 Spoon the mixture into a piping bag fitted with a medium star nozzle and pipe swirls into the tomatoes. Sprinkle with the remaining coriander.

Egg and Bacon on Fried Bread

These miniature "English breakfasts" are an amusing way to serve eggs and bacon as party food.

Makes 12

INGREDIENTS
olive or other vegetable oil, for frying
3–4 medium slices white bread
3 rashers streaky bacon, diced or
   sliced
12 quail's eggs
cherry tomatoes, to garnish

streaky bacon

olive oil

quail's eggs

white bread

COOK'S TIP

The bread and bacon can be cooked in advance and kept warm or reheated in the oven when ready to serve, but the eggs should not be cooked more than 30 minutes before serving.

1 Preheat the oven to 150°C/300°F/ Gas 2. Heat about 1 cm/½ in oil in a heavy medium-sized frying pan. Use a 5 cm/2 in round pastry cutter, to cut 12 rounds from the bread slices.

4 Wipe out the pan and add 30 ml/ 2 tbsp fresh oil to the pan. Break in 4 of the quails' eggs and cook for 2–3 minutes until set. Carefully remove each egg and set on top of the bacon. Continue cooking the eggs in batches, adding a little more oil if necessary, until all are cooked and arranged on the bread rounds.

2 When the oil is hot, but not smoking, add the bread rounds and fry for 2–3 minutes until golden, turning once. Drain on paper towels. You may need to fry the bread in batches. Arrange the bread rounds on a baking sheet in a single layer.

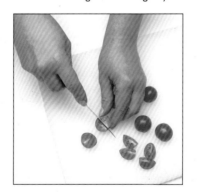

5 Keep the eggs warm in the preheated oven until ready to serve. Cut the cherry tomatoes into quarters. Just before serving arrange the egg-topped bread on a serving dish and garnish each round with a cherry tomato quarter.

3 Pour off all but 15 ml/1 tbsp of oil and add the bacon pieces. Cook for 3–5 minutes, until crisp and golden. Drain well on paper towels, then put a few bacon pieces on each bread round.

VARIATION

If you prefer, instead of frying the eggs, hard boil them by cooking in boiling water for 2–3 minutes. Rinse under cold water and peel. Cut each egg in half and place on the bacon-topped fried bread. Garnish with a piece of chive or parsley leaf.

Herb-stuffed Mini Vegetables

These little hors d'oeuvres are ideal for making in advance and assembled and baked at the last minute.

VARIATION
If you wish, after the first 10 minutes of baking remove from the oven, sprinkle the vegetables with grated parmesan, and grill for 3 minutes.

Makes 30

INGREDIENTS
30 mini vegetables such as courgettes, patty pan squashes, large button mushrooms
fresh basil or parsley, to garnish

FOR THE STUFFING
30 ml/2 tbsp olive oil
1 onion, finely chopped
1 garlic clove, finely chopped
115 g/4 oz button mushrooms, finely chopped
1 courgette, finely chopped
1 red pepper, finely chopped
salt and freshly ground black pepper
65 g/2½ oz/⅓ cup orzo pasta or long grain rice
90 ml/6 tbsp/⅓ cup Italian passata (sieved tomatoes)
2.5 ml/½ tsp dried thyme
120 ml/4 fl oz/½ cup chicken stock
5–10 ml/1–2 tsp chopped fresh basil or parsley
50 g/2 oz mozzarella or fontina cheese, shredded

1 Prepare the stuffing, in a medium-sized frying pan or heavy saucepan. Heat the oil over medium heat. Add the onion and cook for 2–3 minutes until just tender. Stir in the garlic, mushrooms, courgette and red pepper. Season with salt and pepper and cook for 2–3 minutes until the vegetables begin to soften.

2 Stir in the pasta or rice and the passata, then add the thyme and stock and bring to the boil, stirring frequently. Reduce the heat and simmer for 10–12 minutes until all the liquid has evaporated and the mixture is thickened. Remove from the heat and cool slightly. Stir in the basil or parsley and cheese and set aside.

3 Prepare the vegetables, drop the courgettes and patty pan squashes into a large pot of boiling water and cook for 3 minutes. Drain and refresh under cold running water. Trim a thin slice from the length of the courgettes and the bottoms of the squashes so they sit firmly on the plate. Trim 5 mm/¼ in off the tops and scoop out the centres with a small spoon or melon baller; try not to make any holes in the bottom.

courgette
rice
red pepper
squashes
onion
chicken stock
mozzarella cheese
passata
basil
olive oil
thyme
button mushrooms

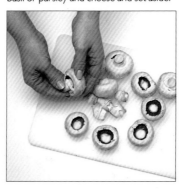

4 Remove the stems from the centre of the mushrooms. If you like, the mushrooms can be blanched like the courgettes or tossed with oil and baked in the oven for 10 minutes at 180°C/350°F/Gas 4. Allow to cool before stuffing.

5 Preheat the oven to 180°C/350°F/Gas 4. Using a teaspoon carefully fill the prepared vegetables with stuffing. Arrange the vegetables in 2 large baking dishes. Pour in enough boiling water just to cover the bottom and prevent the vegetables from sticking.

6 Cover the dishes tightly with foil and bake for 10 minutes. Uncover and bake for about 5 minutes longer, until the filling is hot and bubbling. Remove from the dish to a wire rack or paper towel-lined baking sheet if any water remains. Cool slightly, garnish with basil or parsley and serve warm or at room temperature.

Corn Muffins with Ham

These delicious little muffins are simple to make. If you like, serve them unfilled with a pot of herb butter.

Makes 24

INGREDIENTS

60 g/2 oz/scant ½ cup yellow
   cornmeal
70 g/2½ oz/⅔ cup plain flour
30 ml/2 tbsp sugar
7.5 ml/1½ tsp baking powder
2.5 ml/½ tsp salt
60 g/2 oz/4 tbsp butter, melted
120 ml/4 fl oz/½ cup whipping cream
1 egg, beaten
1–2 jalapeño or other medium-hot
   chillies, seeded and finely chopped
   (optional)
pinch cayenne pepper
butter, for spreading
grainy mustard or mustard with
   honey, for spreading
60 g/2 oz oak-smoked ham

whipping cream

plain
flour

sugar

grainy
mustard

ham

cornmeal

cayenne
pepper

egg

baking
powder

jalapeño chillies

butter

COOK'S TIP

Muffins can be made in advance and stored in air-tight containers. Bring to room temperature or warm slightly before filling and serving.

1 Preheat the oven to 200°C/400°F/Gas 6 and lightly grease a mini muffin pan with 24 4 cm/1½ in cups. In a large bowl combine the cornmeal, flour, sugar, baking powder and salt. In another bowl, whisk together the melted butter, cream, beaten egg, chopped chillies, if using, and the cayenne pepper.

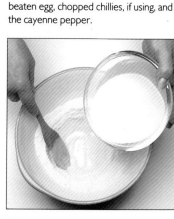

2 Make a well in the cornmeal mixture, pour in the egg mixture and gently stir into the dry ingredients just enough to blend (do not over-beat – the batter does not have to be smooth).

3 Drop 15 ml/1 tbsp batter into each muffin cup and bake for 12–15 minutes, until golden and just firm to the touch. Remove the tray to a wire rack to cool slightly, then turn out the muffins on to the rack, and leave to cool completely.

4 With a sharp knife, split the muffins and spread each bottom half with a little butter and mustard. Cut out small rounds of ham with a round pastry cutter or cut into small squares, and place on the buttered muffins. Sandwich together each muffin with its top and serve.

Buffalo-style Chicken Wings

This fiery-hot fried chicken recipe is said to have originated in the town of Buffalo, New York, but is now popular throughout the USA. Serve it with traditional Blue-cheese Dip and celery sticks.

Makes 48

INGREDIENTS
24 plump chicken wings, tips
    removed
vegetable oil, for frying
salt
75 g/3 oz butter
50 ml/2 oz/¼ cup hot pepper sauce,
    or to taste
15 ml/1 tbsp white or cider vinegar

FOR THE BLUE-CHEESE DIP
115 g/4 oz blue cheese, such as
    Danish blue
120ml/4 fl oz/½ cup mayonnaise
120 ml/4 fl oz/½ cup sour cream
2–3 spring onions, finely chopped
1 garlic clove, finely chopped
15 ml/1 tbsp white or cider vinegar
celery sticks, to serve

1 To make the dip, use a fork to gently mash the blue cheese against the side of a bowl. Add the mayonnaise, sour cream, spring onions, garlic and vinegar and stir together until well blended. Refrigerate until ready to serve.

spring onions · Danish blue cheese · sour cream · vegetable oil · white vinegar · chicken wings · butter · mayonnaise · hot pepper sauce

2 Using kitchen scissors or a sharp knife, cut each wing in half at the joint to make 48 pieces in all.

3 In a large saucepan or wok, heat 5 cm/2 in of oil until hot but not smoking. Fry the chicken wing pieces in small batches for 8–10 minutes until crisp and golden, turning once. Drain on paper towels. Season and arrange in a bowl.

4 In a small saucepan over medium-low heat, melt the butter. Stir in the hot-pepper sauce and vinegar and immediately pour over the chicken, tossing to combine. Serve hot with the blue-cheese dip and celery sticks.

Spicy Sun-dried Tomato Pizza Wedges

These spicy pizza wedges can be made with or without the pepperoni or sausage.

Makes 32

INGREDIENTS
45–60 ml/3–4 tbsp olive oil
2 onions, thinly sliced
2 garlic cloves, chopped
225 g/8 oz mushrooms, sliced
225 g/8 oz canned chopped tomatoes
225 g/8 oz pepperoni or cooked
    Italian-style spicy sausage, chopped
5 ml/1 tsp chilli flakes
5 ml/1 tsp dried oregano
125 g/4 oz sun-dried tomatoes,
    packed in oil, drained and sliced
450 g/1 lb bottled marinated
    artichoke hearts, well drained and
    cut into quarters
225 g/8 oz mozzarella cheese,
    shredded
60 ml/4 tbsp freshly grated Parmesan
    cheese
fresh basil leaves, to garnish
stoned black olives, to garnish

FOR THE DOUGH
1 packet pizza-dough mix
cornmeal, for dusting
virgin olive oil, for brushing and
    drizzling

1 Prepare the pizza dough according to the package directions. Set aside to rise.

2 Prepare the sauce. In a large deep frying pan, heat the oil over medium-high heat. Add the onions and cook for 3–5 minutes until softened. Add the garlic and mushrooms and cook for 3–4 minutes more until the mushrooms begin to colour.

3 Stir in the chopped tomatoes, pepperoni or sausage, chilli flakes and oregano and simmer for 20–30 minutes, stirring frequently, until the sauce is thickened and reduced. Stir in the sun-dried tomatoes and set aside to cool slightly.

onion
cornmeal
grated Parmesan
mushrooms
artichoke hearts
sun-dried tomatoes
virgin olive oil
basil
chilli flakes
pepperoni
black olives
oregano
mozzarella cheese

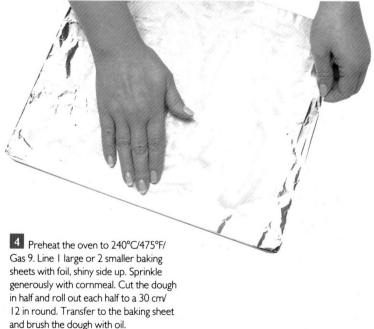

4 Preheat the oven to 240°C/475°F/ Gas 9. Line 1 large or 2 smaller baking sheets with foil, shiny side up. Sprinkle generously with cornmeal. Cut the dough in half and roll out each half to a 30 cm/ 12 in round. Transfer to the baking sheet and brush the dough with oil.

5 Divide the spicy tomato sauce between the dough rounds, spreading to within 1 cm/½ in of the edge. Bake for 5 minutes on the lowest shelf of the oven. Arrange half the artichoke hearts over each, sprinkle evenly with the mozzarella and a little Parmesan. Bake each one in the oven on the bottom shelf for 12–15 minutes longer, until the edge of the crust is crisp and brown and the topping is golden and bubbling. Remove to a wire rack to cool slightly.

6 Slide the pizzas on to a cutting board and cut each into 16 thin wedges. Garnish each wedge with a black olive and basil leaf and serve immediately.

Tortilla Squares

The Spanish tortilla is like the Italian frittata – a flat, baked omelette. Plain or filled, it is always popular.

Makes about 60 squares

INGREDIENTS

60–90 ml/4–6 tbsp olive oil, plus extra for brushing
1 large onion, thinly sliced
350 g/12 oz baking potatoes, thinly sliced
2 garlic cloves, finely chopped
2.5 ml/½ tsp dried thyme
salt and freshly ground black pepper
8 eggs
5–10 ml/1–2 tsp dried oregano or basil
1.25 ml/¼ tsp cayenne pepper or hot pepper sauce, to taste
165 g/5½ oz/1 cup frozen peas, thawed and drained
45–60 ml/2–3 tbsp freshly grated Parmesan cheese
red pepper, to garnish

peas

onion

olive oil

potatoes

garlic

Parmesan cheese

egg

black pepper

oregano

cayenne pepper

thyme

COOK'S TIP

If you like, serve a small bowl of chilli sauce to use as a dip for the tortilla squares.

1 In a large deep, preferably non-stick, frying pan, heat 60 ml/4 tbsp of the oil over a medium heat. Add the onions and potatoes and cook for 8–10 minutes, stirring frequently, until just tender. Add the garlic, thyme, salt and pepper and cook for 2 minutes longer. Remove from the heat and cool slightly.

2 Preheat the oven to 150°C/300°F/Gas 2. Lightly brush a 20 × 30 cm/8 × 12 in square or 25 cm/10 in round baking dish with 30 ml/2 tbsp oil. In a mixing bowl, beat the eggs with the oregano or basil, salt and cayenne pepper until well mixed. Stir in the peas.

3 Spread the cooled potato mixture evenly into the baking dish and carefully pour over the beaten egg and pea mixture. Bake the tortilla for about 40 minutes until just set. Sprinkle with the cheese and bake for another 5 minutes. Remove to a wire rack and cool.

4 Carefully cut the tortilla into 60 small squares. Serve warm or at room temperature with cocktail sticks, and garnished with pieces of red pepper.

Monti Cristo Triangles

These opulent little sandwiches are stuffed with ham, cheese and turkey, dipped in egg, then fried in butter and oil. They are rich and very filling.

Makes 64

INGREDIENTS
16 slices firm-textured thin-sliced
    white bread
120 g/4 oz/½ cup butter, softened
8 slices oak-smoked ham
45–60 ml/3–4 tbsp grainy mustard
8 slices Gruyère or Emmenthal cheese
45–60 ml/3–4 tbsp mayonnaise
8 slices turkey or chicken breast
4–5 eggs
60 ml/2 fl oz/¼ cup milk
salt and white pepper
5 ml/1 tsp Dijon mustard
vegetable oil, for frying
butter, for frying
pimento-stuffed green olives, to
    garnish
parsley leaves, to garnish

oak-smoked ham

turkey breast

white bread

butter *grainy mustard* *egg*

Dijon mustard

stuffed olives

Emmenthal cheese

COOK'S TIP

These sandwiches can be prepared ahead and reheated in a preheated oven at 200°C/400°F/Gas 6 for about 6–8 minutes.

1 Arrange 8 of the bread slices on a work surface and spread with half the softened butter. Lay 1 slice of ham on each slice of bread and spread with a little grainy mustard. Cover with a slice of cheese and spread with a little mayonnaise, then cover with a slice of turkey or chicken breast. Butter the remaining bread slices and use to complete the sandwiches. Cut off the crusts, trimming to an even square.

2 In a large shallow baking dish, beat the eggs, milk, salt and pepper and Dijon mustard until well combined. Soak the sandwiches in the egg mixture on both sides until the egg has been absorbed.

3 Heat about 1 cm/½ in of oil and melted butter in a large heavy frying pan, until hot but not smoking. Gently fry the sandwiches in batches for 4–5 minutes until crisp and golden, turning once. Add more oil and butter as necessary. Drain on paper towels.

4 Transfer the sandwiches to a cutting board and cut each into 4 triangles, then cut each in half again to make 64 triangles. Thread a parsley leaf and olive on to a cocktail stick, then stick into each triangle and serve immediately.

French Country Terrine

This versatile terrine can be served in slices, used to fill sandwiches or cut into small cubes and threaded on to cocktail sticks with tiny gherkins or onions.

COOK'S TIP
The pork can be minced in a hand mincer if you do not have a food processor. Alternatively, ask your butcher to coarsely mince a piece of pork leg or shoulder.

Makes 1 terrine or loaf

INGREDIENTS
450 g/1 lb leeks, trimmed, cut in half lengthways and washed
15 g/½ oz/1 tbsp butter
2–3 garlic cloves, finely chopped
1 kg/2¼ lb lean pork, well trimmed, cut into pieces
150 g/5 oz smoked streaky bacon rashers
7.5 ml/1½ tsp chopped fresh thyme or 5 ml/1 tsp dried thyme
2.5 ml/½ tsp dried sage
1.25 ml/¼ tsp grated nutmeg
2.5 ml/½ tsp quatre épices or allspice
2.5 ml/½ tsp salt
5 ml/1 tsp freshly ground black pepper
2 bay leaves
cherry tomatoes, to garnish

TO SERVE
French country bread or French stick, sliced and toasted
French grainy mustard
pickled gherkins
chicory leaves

1 Thinly slice the leeks. In a large heavy saucepan, melt the butter and stir in the leeks. Cook over low heat, covered, for 10 minutes, stirring occasionally. Stir in the garlic and cook for 5–7 minutes longer, until the leeks are tender. Remove from the heat to cool.

2 Put the pork pieces in the bowl of a food processor (you may need to work in 2 or 3 batches) and process carefully until coarsely chopped. Do not over process. Transfer to a large bowl.

3 Reserve 2 or 3 rashers of bacon and process the remaining slices. Add to the pork mixture with the leeks, thyme, sage, quatre épices, nutmeg, salt and pepper. Using a wooden spoon or your hands, mix until well combined.

streaky bacon

pork

sage

leeks

butter

quatre épices

grainy mustard

nutmeg   French bread

bay leaf   black pepper

4 Preheat the oven to 180°C/350°F/ Gas 4. Grease a heavy, non-stick 1.5 litre/ 2½ pint/6¼ cup terrine or loaf tin. Drape the reserved bacon rashers diagonally across the tin, pressing into the corners. Put the bay leaves down the centre of the tin bottom, then spoon in the terrine mixture, pressing it into the sides and corners. Smooth the top of the terrine and then cover with foil.

5 Put the terrine in a roasting pan and pour in enough boiling water to come half way up the sides of the terrine. Bake for 1¼ hours. Cool completely. Place a foil-covered piece of board, cut to fit, on top of the terrine. Weigh it down with 2 heavy cans or weights and refrigerate overnight.

6 To serve, loosen the edges of the terrine with a knife and turn out onto a serving dish or cutting board. Scrape off any congealed fat or juices and cut into thin slices. Serve on chicory leaves or pieces of toasted French bread, spread with French grainy mustard and gherkins and garnished with cherry tomatoes.

Scandinavian Open Sandwiches

The Swedes and Danes are famous for their open sandwiches, which are often served as part of a *smörgåsbord* – a huge party buffet of both hot and cold dishes.

Makes 16 halves

INGREDIENTS

ROAST BEEF WITH HORSERADISH CREAM
45–60 ml/3–4 tbsp mayonnaise
15 ml/1 tbsp horseradish sauce
2–3 dashes hot pepper sauce
4 slices rye bread
4 slices very rare tender roast beef
diced sweet-and-sour pickled cucumber
watercress, to garnish

GRAVLAX WITH HONEY DILL MUSTARD SAUCE
30–45 ml/2–3 tbsp mayonnaise
10 ml/2 tsp Dijon mustard
15 ml/1 tbsp honey
5 ml/1 tsp vegetable oil
15 ml/1 tbsp chopped fresh dill
4 slices wholemeal bread
4–8 slices gravlax (cured salmon) depending on slice size
cucumber twists, to garnish
dill sprigs, to garnish

SMOKED CHICKEN AND AVOCADO WITH LIME
225 g/8 oz smoked chicken breast, skin removed
1 small ripe avocado, diced
50 ml/2 fl oz/¼ cup garlic mayonnaise
juice of ½ lime
4 slices pumpernickle or black rye bread
5–10 ml/1–2 tsp butter, softened
cucumber twists, to garnish
dill sprigs, to garnish
mint sprigs, to garnish

roast beef
pickled cucumber
watercress
rye bread
horseradish sauce
gravlax
avocado

cucumber *dill* *Dijon mustard*
pumpernickle
smoked chicken breast

COOK'S TIP
All sandwiches are best made immediately before serving. The toppings can be prepared in advance, then assembled at the last minute.

1 To make the Roast Beef with Horseradish, in a small bowl combine the mayonnaise and horseradish together with hot pepper sauce according to taste. Spread the rye bread slices with the horseradish sauce. Arrange the roast beef, in folds for a more attractive appearance, on the bread and cut each slice into 2 triangles. Sprinkle each with a little pickled cucumber, chopped into small cubes and garnish with a sprig of watercress.

2 For the Gravlax with Honey Dill Mustard, in a small bowl combine the mayonnaise, mustard, honey, oil and dill. Reserve 15–20 ml/1–2 tbsp for the garnish. Cut each slice of bread into 2 triangles and spread with the horseradish sauce. Arrange the gravlax on each triangle overlapping slightly, and garnish with cucumber slices and the remaining sauce.

3 For the Smoked Chicken and Avocado, slice the chicken breast. Toss the diced avocado in a bowl with the mayonnaise and lime juice until just blended.

4 Spread the pumpernickle bread slices with a little softened butter and cut each slice into 2 triangles. Arrange a few slices of chicken on the bread and top with a spoonful of the avocado mixture. Garnish with lime slices and a sprig of mint.

Greek Meze with Pitta Crisps

Meze are a selection of Greek hors d'oeuvres, and these three dips are quick and easy to make in a food processor and go well together – serve them with raw vegetables or these wonderful pitta crisps.

INGREDIENTS

FOR THE TZATZIKI (Makes about 750 ml/1¼ pints/3 cups)
1 large cucumber
5 ml/1 tsp salt
600 ml/1 pint/2½ cups thick Greek yogurt
1–2 garlic cloves, finely chopped
30–45 ml/2–3 tbsp chopped fresh mint or 1 tbsp dried mint
15–30 ml/1–2 tbsp virgin olive oil (optional)
mint sprigs, to garnish

FOR THE HUMMUS (Makes about 600 ml/1 pint/2½ cups)
1 × 525 g/19 oz can chickpeas
50 ml/3½ tbsp tahini (sesame paste)
50 ml/3½ tbsp freshly squeezed lemon juice
1–2 garlic cloves, crushed
salt
cayenne pepper, to taste
15–30 ml/1–2 tbsp olive oil
olive or sesame oil, for drizzling
15–30 ml/1–2 tbsp chopped fresh parsley or coriander

FOR THE SMOKY AUBERGINE DIP (Makes about 500 ml/16 fl oz/2 cups)
1 large aubergine (about 450 g/1 lb)
60 ml/4 tbsp freshly squeezed lemon juice
60 ml/4 tbsp tahini or mayonnaise
2–3 garlic cloves, chopped
salt
30 ml/2 tbsp virgin olive oil
30 ml/2 tbsp chopped fresh parsley

cucumber
yogurt
mint
olive oil
chickpeas
tahini
lemon
chopped parsley
cayenne pepper

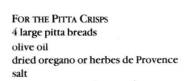

tahini
garlic
aubergine

FOR THE PITTA CRISPS
4 large pitta breads
olive oil
dried oregano or herbes de Provence
salt

1 For the Tzatziki, peel the cucumber and cut lengthways into quarters. Cut out the seeds, chop finely and place in a colander. Sprinkle with the salt and allow to drain for about 1 hour. Pat dry with paper towels. Put the yogurt in a bowl and stir in the drained cucumber, garlic and mint. Slowly blend in the olive oil, if using. Spoon into a serving bowl, garnish with mint and refrigerate.

2 For the Hummus, drain the chickpeas, reserving the liquid. Set aside a few chickpeas for garnishing. Put the remainder in a food processor and add the tahini, lemon juice and garlic. Process until very smooth, scraping down the side of the bowl occasionally. Season with the salt and cayenne pepper and process to blend.

3 With the machine running, slowly pour in 15–30 ml/1–2 tbsp olive oil and some of the reserved chickpea liquid to thin the purée if necessary. Pour into a shallow serving bowl and spread it up the side of the bowl swirling with the back of a spoon. Pour a little extra olive oil or sesame oil in the centre, add the chickpeas and a sprinkle of cayenne pepper. Sprinkle with the chopped parsley or coriander.

4 For the Smoky Aubergine Dip, if possible, barbecue the aubergine over a charcoal fire for about 30 minutes. Alternatively, place on a rack with a tray placed below, in the centre of a preheated oven, 200°C/400°F/Gas 6. Bake for about 30 minutes or until soft, turning frequently. Remove from the oven. When cool enough to handle, scoop out the flesh into the bowl of a food processor. Add the lemon juice, tahini or mayonnaise, garlic, salt to taste, olive oil and 15 ml/1 tbsp of the parsley. Process for 1–2 minutes until very smooth, scraping the sides of the bowl once or twice. Pour into a shallow bowl and garnish with the remaining parsley.

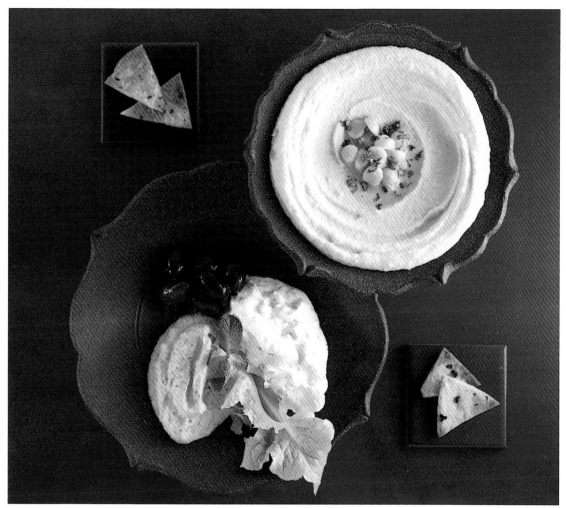

5 For the Pitta Crisps, preheat the oven to 180°C/350°/Gas 4. Split the pittas in half lengthways to form two thin layers. Brush generously with olive oil and sprinkle with a little dried oregano or *herbes de Provence* and a pinch of salt. Cut each in half lengthways, then into triangles and place on 2 large baking sheets. Bake the pitta triangles for 15–20 minutes until golden and crisp. Cool on the baking sheets and then store in an airtight container until ready to serve.

COOK'S TIP

You can, of course, serve these dips with warmed pitta bread, but for parties these crisps are ideal because they don't spoil, and they are cooked in advance, so do make the extra effort – it's worth it!

Corn Fritters with Red Pepper Salsa

The salsa can also be served with grilled chicken or vegetable kebabs. Add the chillies slowly and according to your taste, as they can be very hot.

Makes about 48

INGREDIENTS
corn or other vegetable oil
2 × 225 g/8 oz frozen or canned
    sweetcorn kernals, drained
140 g/5 oz/1 cup plain flour
55 g/2 oz/½ cup cornmeal
250 ml/8 fl oz/1 cup milk
10 ml/2 tsp baking powder
10 ml/2 tsp sugar
5 ml/1 tsp salt
2.5 ml/½ tsp nutmeg
2.5 ml/½ tsp cayenne pepper
4 eggs, lightly beaten
coriander leaves, to garnish

FOR THE SALSA
115 g/4 oz cherry tomatoes, chopped
115 g/4 oz frozen or canned
    sweetcorn kernels, drained
1 red pepper, cored and finely
    chopped
½ small red onion, finely chopped
juice of 1 lemon
30 ml/2 tbsp olive oil
30 ml/2 tbsp chopped fresh coriander
1 to 2 fresh chillies, seeded and finely
    chopped
salt
2.5 ml/½ tsp sugar

1 Prepare the Salsa at least 2 hours ahead. Combine the ingredients in a medium-sized bowl, crushing them lightly with the back of a spoon to release juices. Cover and refrigerate until ready to use.

red onion
sweetcorn
red pepper

egg
cornmeal
lemon
chilli
chopped coriander
milk
cherry tomatoes
olive oil
cayenne pepper
nutmeg

2 In a medium-sized bowl combine 30 ml/2 tbsp of the oil with the sweetcorn, flour, cornmeal, milk, baking powder, sugar, salt, nutmeg, cayenne pepper and eggs, until just blended; do not overbeat. If the batter is too stiff stir in a little more milk or water.

3 In a large heavy-based frying pan, heat 1 cm/½ in oil until hot but not smoking. Drop tablespoonsful of batter into the hot oil and cook for 3 to 4 minutes until golden, turning once. Drain on paper towels. Arrange on baking sheets and keep warm for up to 1 hour in an oven, at 170°C/325°F/Gas 3.

4 Arrange the corn fritters on a serving plate. Top each with a spoonful of salsa and garnish with a coriander leaf. Serve hot or warm.

COOK'S TIP
The salsa can be made up to a day in advance. Keep in the fridge, covered.

Mini Sausage Rolls

These miniature versions of old-fashioned sausage rolls are always popular – the Parmesan cheese gives them an extra special flavour.

Makes about 48

INGREDIENTS

15 g/½ oz/1 tbsp butter
1 onion, finely chopped
350 g/12 oz good quality sausage meat
15 ml/1 tbsp dried mixed herbs such as oregano, thyme, sage, tarragon or dill
salt and pepper
25 g/1 oz finely chopped pistachio nuts (optional)
350 g/12 oz puff pastry
60–90 ml/4–6 tbsp freshly grated Parmesan cheese
1 egg, lightly beaten, for glazing
poppy seeds, sesame seeds, fennel seeds or aniseeds, for sprinkling

sausage meat
dried mixed herbs
puff pastry
egg
Parmesan cheese
fennel seeds
sesame seeds
pistachio nuts
poppy seeds
onion
butter

VARIATION

Filo pastry can be used instead of puff pastry for a very light effect. Depending on the size of the filo sheets, cut into 8 pieces 25 × 7.5 cm/ 10 × 3 in. Brush 4 of the sheets with a little melted butter or vegetable oil and place a second pastry sheet on top. Place one sausage log on each of the four layered sheets and roll up and bake as above.

1 In a small frying pan, over a medium heat, melt the butter. Add the onion and cook for about 5 minutes, until softened. Remove from the heat and cool. Put the onion, sausage meat, herbs, salt and pepper and nuts (if using) in a mixing bowl and stir together until blended.

2 Divide the sausage mixture into 4 equal portions and roll into thin sausages about 25 cm/10 in long. Set aside.

3 On a lightly floured surface, roll out the pastry to about 3 mm/⅛ in thick. Cut the pastry into 4 strips 25 × 7.5 cm/ 10 × 3 in long. Place a long sausage on each pastry strip and sprinkle each with a little Parmesan cheese.

4 Brush one long edge of each of the pastry strips with the egg glaze and roll up to enclose each sausage. Set them seam-side down and press gently to seal. Brush each with the egg glaze and sprinkle with one type of seeds. Repeat with remaining pastry strips and different seeds.

5 Preheat the oven to 220°C/425°F/ Gas 7. Lightly grease a large baking sheet. Cut each of the pastry logs into 2.5 cm/ 1 in lengths and arrange on the baking sheet. Bake for 15 minutes until the pastry is crisp and brown. Serve warm or at room temperature.

Smoked Trout Mousse in Cucumber Cups

This delicious creamy mousse can be made in advance and kept for 2–3 days in the refrigerator. Serve it in crunchy cucumber cups, or simply with crudités.

Makes about 24

INGREDIENTS
120 g/4 oz/⅔ cup cream cheese, softened
2 spring onions, chopped
15–30 ml/1–2 tbsp, chopped fresh dill or parsley
5 ml/1 tsp horseradish sauce
225 g/8 oz smoked trout fillets, flaked and any fine bones removed
30–60 ml/2–4 tbsp double cream
salt
cayenne pepper, to taste
2 cucumbers
dill sprigs, to garnish

spring onions

cucumber

smoked trout

double cream

cream cheese

cayenne pepper

horseradish sauce

dill

VARIATION
For Smoked Salmon Mousse use smoked salmon pieces instead of smoked trout.

1 Put the cream cheese, spring onions, dill and horseradish sauce into the bowl of a food processor and process until well blended. Add the trout and process until smooth, scraping down the side of the bowl once. With the machine running, pour in the cream until a soft mousse-like mixture forms. Season, turn into a bowl and refrigerate for 15 minutes.

2 Using a canelle knife or vegetable peeler, score the length of each cucumber to create a striped effect. Cut each cucumber into 2 cm/¾ in thick rounds. Using a small spoon or melon baller, scoop out the seeds from the centre of each round.

3 Spoon the mousse into a piping bag fitted with a medium star nozzle and pipe swirls of the mixture into the cucumber rounds. Refrigerate until ready to serve. Garnish each with a small sprig of dill.

Carpaccio Rolls with Anchovy Mayonnaise

This famous hors d'oeuvre of raw beef makes an extravagant but delicious treat.

Makes about 24

INGREDIENTS

225 g/8 oz fillet of beef, cut from the narrow end, and frozen for 1 hour
60 ml/4 tbsp virgin olive oil
15 ml/1 tbsp lemon juice
freshly ground black pepper
rocket or flat-leaf parsley, to garnish
capers, to garnish

FOR THE ANCHOVY MAYONNAISE
4–6 anchovy fillets
250 ml/8 fl oz/1 cup home-made or good quality mayonnaise
15 ml/1 tbsp capers, rinsed, drained and chopped
1 small garlic clove, crushed
30 ml/2 tbsp freshly grated Parmesan cheese

endive leaves or short celery sticks, to serve

lemon   Parmesan cheese

fillet of beef

anchovy fillets

virgin olive oil

mayonnaise

capers   garlic

1 For the Anchovy Mayonnaise, in a medium-sized bowl, mash the anchovy fillets with a fork, then beat in the mayonnaise, capers, garlic and Parmesan cheese until well blended.

2 Slice the beef into as many wafer-thin pieces as possible and arrange flat on a baking sheet. Brush each piece with the olive oil and sprinkle with a little lemon juice and black pepper.

3 Place about half a teaspoon of Anchovy Mayonnaise in the centre of each beef slice and fold into quarters, or roll up.

4 To serve, place a rocket leaf at the bottom of an endive leaf and place a rolled or folded up slice of beef on top. Sprinkle with a few capers if you like. If you prefer, skewer each beef parcel with a cocktail stick and serve on its own.

Spicy Crab Cakes

These are miniature versions of a classic American speciality. Use fresh crab meat if your budget allows.

Makes about 30

INGREDIENTS

225 g/8 oz crab meat, drained and picked over
75 g/3 oz/1½ cups fresh white breadcrumbs
2 spring onions, finely chopped
15–30 ml/1–2 tbsp chopped fresh dill or parsley
1 egg, lightly beaten
50 ml/2 fl oz/¼ cup mayonnaise
15 ml/1 tbsp Dijon mustard
15–30 ml/1–2 tbsp lemon juice
salt
1 small green chilli, seeded and chopped (optional)
2–3 dashes hot pepper sauce
fine dried breadcrumbs, for coating
vegetable oil, for frying

FOR THE SEAFOOD COCKTAIL SAUCE
115 ml/4 fl oz/½ cup horseradish sauce
15–30 ml/1–2 tbsp mayonnaise
50 ml/2 fl oz/¼ cup tomato ketchup
lemon juice, to taste

crab meat   breadcrumbs
chilli pepper
egg   mayonnaise   Dijon mustard
parsley   tomato ketchup   horseradish sauce
hot pepper sauce   spring onions
lemon

1 For the Seafood Cocktail Sauce, in a small bowl, combine all the ingredients and mix well. Cover and refrigerate. For the crab cakes, in a large bowl, combine all the ingredients, except the oil and dried breadcrumbs.

2 Using a small ice-cream scoop or teaspoon, form the mixture into walnut-sized balls. Place on a baking sheet.

3 Put the dried breadcrumbs in a shallow plate and coat the crab balls, a few at a time, rolling to cover completely. Place on a baking sheet and flatten each ball slightly until 1 cm/½ in thick. Refrigerate for 30 minutes or longer.

4 In a large heavy frying pan heat 1 cm/½ in of oil, until hot but not smoking. Fry the crab cakes, in batches, for about 2 minutes until crisp and golden, turning once. Serve hot or warm with the sauce.

Smoked Salmon Nests on Wild Rice Pancakes

The nutty flavour of wild rice provides a perfect foil to the smoky richness of the salmon, in this elegant hors d'oeuvre.

Makes about 24

INGREDIENTS
225 g/8 oz smoked salmon
45–60 ml/3–4 tbsp creamed
   horseradish sauce
fresh chives or dill, to garnish

FOR THE WILD RICE PANCAKES
70 g/2½ oz/½ cup plain flour
salt and white pepper
1 egg, lightly beaten
60 ml/2 fl oz/¼ cup milk
200 g/7 oz/1⅓ cups cooked wild rice
30 ml/2 tbsp chopped chives or dill
vegetable oil, for frying

vegetable oil

milk

egg

horseradish sauce

plain flour

chives

smoked salmon   *wild rice*

1 Prepare the Wild Rice Pancakes, sift the flour, salt and pepper into a medium-sized bowl and make a well in the centre. Put the egg and milk in the well and, using a wire whisk or electric beater on slow speed, gradually bring in the flour from the edges to form a smooth batter. Stir in the wild rice and chives or dill.

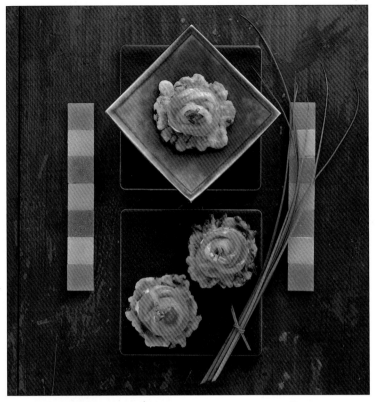

VARIATION

The same effect can be achieved more simply by making little bread rounds instead of pancakes. Cut out 5 cm/2 in rounds from white or brown sliced bread and toast briefly on both sides before adding the topping.

2 In a large heavy frying pan heat 30–45 ml/2–3 tbsp oil over a medium-high heat until very hot. Drop tablespoonsful of the batter into the pan and flatten slightly. Cook for 2–3 minutes until golden, turning once. Drain on paper towels and keep warm.

3 With a sharp knife, cut the smoked salmon into thin strips. Spoon a little horseradish cream onto each pancake and top with a pile of salmon strips twisting to form a nest. If you like, garnish with extra dollops of horseradish cream and fresh chives or dill.

Foie Gras Pâté in Filo Cups

This is an extravagantly rich hors d'oeuvre – save it for a special occasion.

Makes about 24

INGREDIENTS
3–6 sheets fresh or defrosted filo pastry
45 g/1½ oz/3 tbsp butter, melted
225 g/8 oz tinned foie gras pâté or other fine liver pâté, at room temperature
60 g/2 oz/4 tbsp butter, softened
30–45 ml/2–3 tbsp Cognac or brandy (optional)
chopped pistachios, to garnish

filo pastry

foie gras pâté

pistachio nuts

butter

Cognac

1 Preheat the oven to 200°C/400°F/ Gas 6. Grease a bun tray with 24 × 4 cm/ 1½ in cups. Stack the filo sheets on a work surface and cut into 6 cm/2½ in squares. Cover with a damp towel.

2 Keeping the rest of the filo squares covered, place one square on a work surface and brush lightly with melted butter, then turn and brush the other side.

Butter a second square and place it over the first at an angle. Butter a third square and place at an angle over the first two sheets to form an uneven edge.

3 Press the layers into the cup of the bun tray. Continue with the remaining pastry and butter until all the cups are filled.

4 Bake the filo cups for 4–6 minutes until crisp and golden, then remove and cool in the pan for 5 minutes. Carefully remove each filo cup to a wire rack and cool completely.

5 In a small bowl, beat the pâté with the softened butter until smooth and well blended. Add the Cognac or brandy to taste, if using. Spoon into a piping bag fitted with a medium star nozzle and pipe a swirl into each cup. Sprinkle with pistachio nuts. Refrigerate until ready to serve.

COOK'S TIP
The pâté and pastry are best eaten soon after preparation. If preparing ahead and refrigerating, be sure to bring back to room temperature before serving.

Grilled Asparagus Tips with Easy Hollandaise Sauce

Delicate asparagus tips and buttery rich Hollandaise Sauce make a classic combination and a delicious treat.

Makes 24

INGREDIENTS
24 large asparagus spears
oil, for brushing
freshly grated Parmesan cheese, for
  sprinkling

FOR THE HOLLANDAISE SAUCE
175 g/6 oz/¾ cup butter, cut into
  pieces
2 egg yolks
15 ml/1 tbsp lemon juice
15 ml/1 tbsp water
salt and cayenne pepper

asparagus

egg yolks

butter

cayenne pepper

lemon

lemon juice

COOK'S TIP
Keep the Hollandaise Sauce warm by storing it in a vacuum flask until ready to serve.

1 Prepare the Hollandaise Sauce, melt the butter in a small saucepan and skim off any foam which bubbles to the top.

2 Put the egg yolks, lemon juice and water into a blender or a food processor. Season with salt and cayenne pepper and blend or process to mix. With the machine running, slowly pour in the hot butter in a thin stream; do not pour in the milky solids on the bottom of the pan.

3 Using a vegetable peeler, peel the asparagus spears. Cut off the stalks to leave tips of about 12.5 cm/5 in. (Reserve the stalks for another dish such as Stir-fried Vegetable Cups.)

4 Cook the tips in boiling salted water for 2–3 minutes until just tender; do not overcook. Refresh under cold water to stop them cooking, then cover until ready to serve.

5 Preheat the grill. Line a baking sheet with foil and brush each asparagus tip with a little oil. Sprinkle each tip with a little Parmesan cheese, then grill for 2–3 minutes, turning once. Arrange the asparagus on a plate, and serve with the Hollandaise Sauce for dipping.

VARIATION

Wrap each asparagus tip in a thin strip of bacon or Parma ham and brush with oil before grilling. If you like cut the remainder of the asparagus spears into 7.5 cm/3 in pieces and grill them, for slightly longer, as well.

Marinated Mussels

This is an ideal recipe to prepare and arrange well in advance. Remove from the refrigerator 15 minutes before serving to allow the flavours to develop.

Makes 48

INGREDIENTS

1 kilo/2.2 lb mussels, large if possible
175 ml/6 fl oz/¾ cup dry white wine
1 garlic clove, well crushed
freshly ground black pepper
120 ml/4 fl oz/½ cup olive oil
50 ml/2 fl oz/¼ cup lemon juice
5 ml/1 tsp hot chilli flakes
2.5 ml/½ tsp mixed spice
15 ml/1 tbsp Dijon mustard
10 ml/2 tsp sugar
5 ml/1 tsp salt
15–30 ml/1–2 tbsp chopped fresh dill
   or coriander
15 ml/1 tbsp capers, diced, drained
   and chopped if large

lemon   mussels

sugar

            olive oil

mixed spice   capers

garlic

Dijon
mustard

            dill

      hot chilli
      flakes

1 With a stiff kitchen brush, under running cold water, scrub the mussels to remove any sand and barnacles; pull out and remove any beards. Discard any open shells that will not shut when tapped.

3 In a large bowl combine the olive oil, lemon juice, chilli flakes, mixed spice, Dijon mustard, sugar, salt, chopped dill or coriander and capers.

4 Discard any mussels with closed shells. With a small sharp knife, carefully remove remaining mussels from their shells, reserving 48 shells for serving. Add the mussels to the marinade. Toss the mussels to coat well, then cover and refrigerate for 6 to 8 hours or overnight, stirring gently from time to time.

COOK'S TIP

Mussels can be prepared ahead and marinated for up to 24 hours. To serve, arrange the mussel shells on a bed of crushed ice, well-washed seaweed or even coarse salt to stop them wobbling on the plate.

2 In a large casserole or saucepan over high heat, bring to the boil the white wine with the garlic and freshly ground black pepper. Add the mussels and cover. Reduce the heat to medium and simmer for 2 to 4 minutes until the shells open, stirring occasionally.

5 With a teaspoon, place one mussel with a little marinade in each shell. Arrange on a platter and cover until ready to serve.

A Trio of Tartlets

Tender pastry topped with luscious ingredients always look irresistible and taste even better. Vary the toppings according to the occasion.

Makes about 24

INGREDIENTS
175 g/6 oz/1⅓ cups flour
2.5 ml/½ tsp salt
75 g/3 oz/6 tbsp butter, cut into
  pieces
1 egg yolk beaten with 30–45 ml/2–3
  tbsp cold water

FOR THE SCRAMBLED EGG AND CAVIAR
15 ml/1 tbsp butter
2 eggs, lightly beaten
salt and white pepper
15 ml/1 tbsp double cream or crème
  fraîche
15–30 ml/1–2 tbsp caviar or lumpfish
  caviar

FOR THE SMOKED SALMON AND LEEK
120 ml/4 oz/½ cup double cream
1 leek, split lengthways, washed and
  thinly sliced
salt and freshly ground black pepper
pinch of nutmeg
115 g/4 oz smoked salmon, sliced very
  thinly
dill sprigs, to garnish

FOR THE ASPARAGUS AND BRIE
15 ml/1 tbsp butter
6 asparagus stalks cut into 4 cm/1½ in
  pieces
salt
50 g/2 oz Brie, rind removed and
  sliced

flour

salt

eggs

caviar

double cream

butter

smoked salmon

leek

nutmeg

Brie

asparagus

1 Prepare the pastry, put the flour, salt and butter into the bowl of a food processor and process carefully, until the mixture resembles fine crumbs. Reserve 15 ml/1 tbsp of the egg mixture. With the processor running, pour in the remaining egg mixture until the dough just begins to come together (do not allow it to form a ball or it may toughen). If the dough is too dry add a little more water and process briefly again. Turn the dough on to a piece of clear film and use the film to push it together and flatten to form a disc shape. Wrap tightly, refrigerate for 1½ hours.

2 On a lightly floured surface, roll out the pastry to a 3 mm/⅛ in thickness. Lay out about 12 5 cm/2 in tartlet tins. Lay the pastry over the tins and press out. Reroll the trimmings and repeat. Line 24 cases, then prick the bases with a fork and refrigerate for 30 minutes.

3 Preheat the oven to 190°C/375°F/ Gas 5. Put a small piece of crumbled foil into each case and place on a baking sheet. Bake for 6–8 minutes until the edges are golden. Remove the foil and brush each pastry base with a little of the reserved egg mixture. Bake for 2 minutes until dry. Transfer to a wire rack to cool.

4 Prepare the fillings, for the Scrambled Egg and Caviar, melt the butter in a small frying pan over medium-low heat. Season the eggs with salt and white pepper and add to the pan. Cook the eggs slowly, stirring constantly, until smooth and just set. Remove from the heat and stir in the cream or crème fraîche. Spoon into 8 of the cases. Just before serving, garnish each tartlet with a pinch of caviar. Serve warm or at room temperature.

5 For the Smoked Salmon and Leek, bring the cream to a simmer in a medium saucepan over medium heat. Add the leeks and cook, stirring frequently, until just tender and the cream is completely reduced. Season with salt, pepper and a pinch of nutmeg. Spoon into 8 of the cases and top with smoked salmon strips and sprigs of dill just before serving. Serve warm or at room temperature.

6 For the Asparagus and Brie, melt the butter in a medium-sized frying pan over medium-high heat. Add the asparagus pieces and stir-fry for 2–3 minutes until tender. Divide among the remaining tartlets and sprinkle each with a little salt. Divide the Brie among the tartlets. Just before serving, return to the oven for 1–2 minutes until the Brie softens. Serve straight away before the cheese hardens.

COOK'S TIP

If you do not have 24 tartlet tins, you will need to work in batches. Divide the dough in half or quarters and refrigerate the portion you are not using immediately.

Hazelnut Sablés with Goat's Cheese and Strawberries

Sablés are little French biscuits, made from egg yolk and butter. Crisp and slightly sweet, they contrast perfectly with the tangy goat's cheese and juicy strawberries.

Makes about 24

INGREDIENTS
75 g/3 oz/6 tbsp butter, at room
   temperature
140 g/5 oz/1 cup plain flour
75 g/3 oz/6 tbsp blanched hazelnuts,
   lightly toasted and ground
30 ml/2 tbsp caster sugar
2 egg yolks beaten with 30–45 ml/2–3
   tbsp water
120 g/4 oz goat's cheese
4–6 large strawberries, cut into small
   pieces
chopped hazelnuts, to decorate

goat's cheese   *strawberries*

ground hazelnuts

butter

chopped hazelnuts

egg yolks

flour

VARIATION
These sablés are ideal served with fruit. Beat 75 g/3 oz cream cheese with 15 ml/1 tbsp icing sugar and a little lemon or orange zest. Spread a little on the sablé and top with a few pieces of sliced kiwi fruit, peach, nectarine and a few raspberries or cut-up strawberries.

1 Make the pastry, put the butter, flour, ground hazelnuts, sugar and beaten egg yolks into the bowl of a food processor and process until a smooth dough forms.

2 Scrape the dough out on to a sheet of clear film and use the film to shape the dough into a log about 4 cm/1 ½ in in diameter. Wrap tightly and refrigerate for 2 hours or overnight until very firm.

3 Preheat the oven to 200°C/400°F/ Gas 6 and line a large baking sheet with non-stick baking parchment. With a sharp knife slice the dough into 5 mm/¼ in thick rounds and arrange on the baking sheet. Bake for 7–10 minutes until golden brown. Remove to a wire rack to cool and crisp slightly.

4 On a plate, crumble the goat's cheese into small pieces. Mound a little goat's cheese on to each sablé, top with a piece of strawberry and sprinkle with a few hazelnuts. Serve warm.

Rich Chocolate and Fruit Fondue

This sumptuous fruit fondue, with its rich, delicious sauce, makes a lavish finish to a party.

Makes 350 ml/12 fl oz/1½ cups

INGREDIENTS
a selection of mixed fruit, such as kumquats, apple, peach and pear slices, banana slices, clementine segments, seedless grapes, cherries, peeled lychees, mango and papaya cubes, cut figs and plums
lemon juice

FOR THE CHOCOLATE
225 g/8 oz good quality plain chocolate, chopped
30 ml/2 tbsp golden syrup
120 ml/4 fl oz/½ cup whipping cream
30–45 ml/2–3 tbsp brandy or orange-liqueur

peach
clementine *strawberries* *cherries*
fig *lychees*
kumquat *plum* *grapes*
whipping cream
plain chocolate *brandy* *lemon juice*

1 Arrange the fruits in an attractive pattern on a large serving dish. Brush any cut-up fruit such as apples, pears or banana with lemon juice to prevent darkening. Cover and refrigerate until ready to serve.

2 In a medium-sized saucepan over medium-low heat, combine the chopped chocolate, golden syrup and whipping cream. Stir until the chocolate is melted and smooth. Remove from the heat and stir in the brandy or liqueur. Poor into a serving bowl and serve with the chilled fruits and cocktail sticks.

VARIATION
You could also use small biscuits for dipping as well as, or instead of, the pieces of fruit.

Prawn Toasts

These crunchy sesame-topped toasts are simple to prepare using a food processor for the prawn paste.

Makes 64

INGREDIENTS
225 g/8 oz cooked, shelled prawns,
    well drained and dried
1 egg white
2 spring onions, chopped
5 ml/1 tsp chopped fresh root ginger
1 garlic clove, chopped
5 ml/1 tsp cornflour
2.5 ml/½ tsp salt
2.5 ml/½ tsp sugar
2–3 dashes hot pepper sauce
8 slices firm textured white bread
60–75 ml/4–5 tbsp sesame seeds
vegetable oil, for frying
spring onion pompom, to garnish

bread
vegetable oil
egg white
sesame seeds
root ginger
sugar
garlic
prawns
cornflour
spring onions
hot pepper sauce

1 Put the first 9 ingredients in the bowl of a food processor and process until the mixture forms a smooth paste, scraping down the side of the bowl occasionally.

2 Spread the prawn paste evenly over the bread slices, then sprinkle over the sesame seeds, pressing to make them stick. Remove the crusts, then cut each slice diagonally into 4 triangles, then cut each in half again to make 64 in total.

3 Heat 5 cm/2 in vegetable oil in a heavy saucepan or wok, until hot but not smoking. Fry the prawn-coated triangles for 30–60 seconds, turning once. Drain on paper towels and serve hot.

COOK'S TIP

You can prepare these in advance and heat them up in a hot oven before serving. Make sure they are crisp and properly heated through though, they won't be nearly as enjoyable if there's no crunch!

Thai-fried Vegetables in Wonton Cups

These crispy cups are an ideal way to serve stir-fried vegetables; use your imagination to vary the fillings.

Makes 24

INGREDIENTS

30 ml/2 tbsp vegetable oil, plus extra for greasing
24 small wonton wrappers
120 ml/4 fl oz/½ cup Hoi Sin sauce or plum sauce (optional)
5 ml/1 tsp sesame oil
1 garlic clove, finely chopped
1 cm/½ in piece fresh root ginger, finely chopped
5 cm/2 in piece of lemon grass, crushed
6–8 asparagus spears, cut into 3 cm/1¼ in pieces
8–10 baby sweetcorn, cut in half lengthways
1 small red pepper, seeded and cut into short slivers
15–30 ml/1–2 tbsp sugar
30 ml/2 tbsp soy sauce
juice of 1 lime
5–10 ml/1–2 tsp Chinese-style chilli sauce (or to taste)
1 tsp *huac nam* or Thai or other fish sauce

lemon grass

red pepper

Hoi Sin sauce

wonton wrappers

vegetable oil

baby sweetcorn

asparagus

sesame oil

soy sauce

lime

garlic

3 Add the sugar, soy sauce, lime juice, chilli sauce and fish sauce and toss well to coat. Stir-fry for 30 seconds longer.

4 Spoon an equal amount of vegetable mixture into each of the prepared wonton cups and serve hot.

1 Preheat the oven to 180°C/350°F/ Gas 4. Lightly grease 24 4 cm/1½ in bun tins. Press 1 wonton wrapper into each cup, turning the edges up to form a cup shape. Bake for 8–10 minutes, until crisp and golden. Carefully remove to a wire rack to cool. If you like, brush each cup with a little Hoi Sin or plum sauce (this will help keep the cups crisp if preparing them in advance).

2 In a wok or large frying pan, heat 30 ml/2 tbsp vegetable oil and the sesame oil until very hot. Add the garlic, ginger and lemon grass and stir-fry for 15 seconds until fragrant. Add the asparagus, sweetcorn and red pepper pieces and stir-fry for 2 minutes until tender crisp.

Chicken Satay with Peanut Sauce

These skewers of marinated chicken can be prepared in advance and served at room temperature. Beef, pork or even lamb fillet can be used instead of chicken if you prefer.

Makes about 24

INGREDIENTS
450 g/1 lb boneless, skinless chicken breasts
sesame seeds, for sprinkling
red pepper, to garnish

FOR THE MARINADE
90 ml/6 tbsp vegetable oil
60 ml/4 tbsp tamari or light soy sauce
60 ml/4 tbsp fresh lime juice
2.5 cm/½ in piece fresh root ginger, peeled and chopped
3–4 garlic cloves
30 ml/2 tbsp light brown sugar
5 ml/1 tsp Chinese-style chilli sauce or 1 small red chilli pepper, seeded and chopped
30 ml/2 tbsp fresh chopped coriander

FOR THE PEANUT SAUCE
30 ml/2 tbsp smooth peanut butter
30 ml/2 tbsp soy sauce
15 ml/1 tbsp sesame or vegetable oil
2 spring onions, chopped
2 garlic cloves
15–30 ml/1–2 tbsp fresh lime or lemon juice
15 ml/1 tbsp brown sugar

1 Prepare the marinade. Place all the marinade ingredients in the bowl of a food processor or blender and process until smooth and well blended, scraping down sides of the bowl once. Pour into a shallow dish and set aside.

red pepper   *ginger*   *vegetable oil*
brown sugar
soy sauce
coriander
chilli sauce
lime
spring onions
garlic
sesame oil
sesame seeds
chicken breast

2 Into the same food processor or blender, put all the Peanut Sauce ingredients and process until well blended. If the sauce is too thick add a little water and process again. Pour into a small bowl and cover until ready to serve.

4 Add the chicken pieces to the marinade in the dish. Toss well to coat, cover and marinate for 3–4 hours in a cool place, or overnight in a refrigerator.

3 Put the chicken breasts in the freezer for 5 minutes to firm. Slice the chicken breasts in half horizontally, then into thin strips. Cut the strips into 2 cm/¾ in pieces.

5 Preheat the grill. Line a baking sheet with foil and brush lightly with oil. Thread 2–3 pieces of marinated chicken on to skewers and sprinkle with the sesame seeds. Grill for 4–5 minutes until golden, turning once. Serve with the Peanut Sauce, and a garnish of red pepper strips.

COOK'S TIP
When using metal skewers, look for flat ones which prevent the food from spinning around. If using wooden skewers, be sure to soak them in cold water for at least 30 minutes, to prevent them from burning.

Lamb Tikka

Creamy yogurt and nuts go wonderfully with the spices in these little Indian meatballs.

Makes about 20

INGREDIENTS

450 g/1 lb lamb fillet
2 spring onions, chopped

FOR THE MARINADE

350 ml/12 fl oz/1½ cups natural yogurt
15 ml/1 tbsp ground almonds, cashews or peanuts
15 ml/1 tbsp vegetable oil
2–3 garlic cloves, finely chopped
juice of 1 lemon
5 ml/1 tsp garam masala or curry powder
2.5 ml/½ tsp ground cardamom
1.25 ml/¼ tsp cayenne pepper
15–30 ml/1–2 tbsp chopped fresh mint

spring onions

lamb fillet *ground almonds* *natural yogurt*

lemon *garam masala* *cayenne pepper*

ground cardamom *vegetable oil*

garlic

mint

1 Prepare the marinade, in a medium-sized bowl, stir together all the ingredients except the lamb. In a separate small bowl, reserve about 120 ml/4 fl oz/½ cup of the mixture to use as a dipping sauce.

2 Cut the lamb into small pieces and put in the bowl of a food processor with the spring onions. Process, using the pulse action until the meat is finely chopped. Add 30–45 ml/2–3 tbsp of the marinade and process again.

3 Test to see if the mixture holds together by pinching a little between your fingertips. Add a little more marinade if necessary, but do not make the mixture too wet and soft.

4 With moistened palms, form the meat mixture into slightly oval-shaped balls about 4 cm/1½ in long and arrange in a shallow baking dish. Spoon over the remaining marinade and refrigerate the meat balls for 8–10 hours or overnight.

5 Preheat the grill and line a baking sheet with foil. Thread each meatball on to a skewer and arrange on the baking sheet. Grill for 4–5 minutes, turning occasionally, until crisp and golden on all sides. Serve with the reserved marinade/dipping sauce.

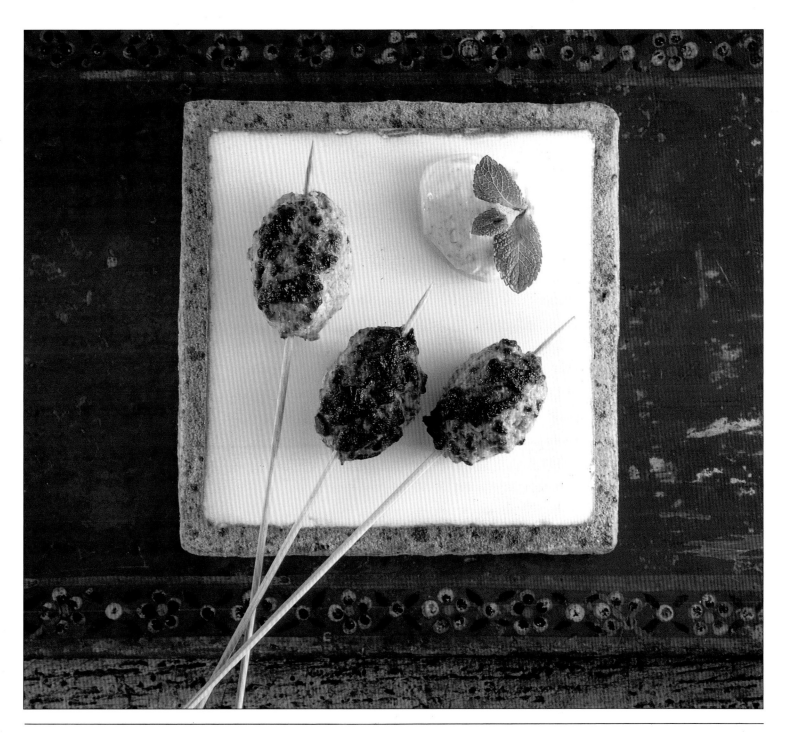

Smoked Duck Wontons with Spicy Mango Sauce

These Chinese-style wontons are easy to make using ready-cooked smoked duck or chicken, or even left-overs from the Sunday roast.

Makes about 40

INGREDIENTS
15 ml/1 tbsp light soy sauce
5 ml/1 tsp sesame oil
2 spring onions, finely chopped
grated zest of ½ orange
5 ml/1 tsp brown sugar
275 g/10 oz/1½ cups chopped
 smoked duck
about 40 small wonton wrappers
15 ml/1 tbsp vegetable oil

FOR THE SPICY MANGO SAUCE
30 ml/2 tbsp vegetable oil
5 ml/1 tsp ground cumin
2.5 ml/½ tsp ground cardamom
1.25 ml/¼ tsp ground cinnamon
250 ml/8 fl oz/1 cup mango purée
 (about 1 large mango)
15 ml/1 tbsp clear honey
2.5 ml/½ tsp Chinese chilli sauce (or
 to taste)
15 ml/1 tbsp cider vinegar
snipped fresh chives, to garnish

mango
wonton wrappers
spring onions
soy sauce
brown sugar
smoked duck
cardamom
cumin
cinnamon
sesame oil
chilli sauce
cider vinegar

COOK'S TIP
Wonton wrappers, available in some large supermarkets and Asian markets, are sold in 450 g/1 lb packages and can be stored in the freezer almost indefinitely. Remove as many as you need, keeping the rest frozen.

1 Prepare the sauce. In a medium-sized saucepan, heat the oil over medium-low heat. Add the spices and cook for about 3 minutes, stirring constantly.

2 Stir in the mango purée, honey, chilli sauce and vinegar. Remove from the heat and cool. Pour into a bowl and cover until ready to serve.

3 Prepare the wonton filling. In a large bowl, mix together the soy sauce, sesame oil, spring onions, orange zest and brown sugar until well blended. Add the duck and toss to coat well.

4 Place a teaspoonful of the duck mixture in the centre of each wonton wrapper. Brush the edges lightly with water and then draw them up to the centre, twisting to seal and forming a pouch shape.

5 Preheat the oven to 190°F/375°C/ Gas 6. Line a large baking sheet with foil and brush lightly with oil. Arrange the wontons on the baking sheet and bake for 10–12 minutes until crisp and golden. Serve with the Spicy Mango Sauce. If you wish, tie each wonton with a fresh chive.

Tandoori Chicken Sticks

This aromatic chicken dish is traditionally baked in a special clay oven called a tandoor.

Makes about 25

INGREDIENTS
450 g/1 lb boneless, skinless chicken
   breasts

FOR THE CORIANDER YOGURT
250 ml/8 fl oz/1 cup natural yogurt
30 ml/2 tbsp whipping cream
½ cucumber, peeled, seeded and
   finely chopped
15–30 ml/1–2 tbsp fresh chopped
   coriander or mint
salt and freshly ground black pepper

FOR THE MARINADE
175 ml/6 fl oz/¾ cup natural yogurt
5 ml/1 tsp garam masala or curry
   powder
1.25 ml/¼ tsp ground cumin
1.25 ml/¼ tsp ground coriander
1.25 ml/¼ tsp cayenne pepper (or to
   taste)
5 ml/1 tsp tomato purée
1–2 garlic cloves, finely chopped
2.5 cm/½ in piece fresh root ginger,
   peeled and finely chopped
grated zest and juice of ½ lemon
15–30 ml/1–2 tbsp fresh chopped
   coriander or mint

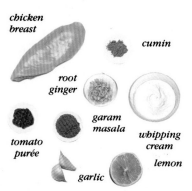

chicken breast
cumin
root ginger
garam masala
tomato purée
whipping cream
garlic
lemon
cucumber
natural yogurt

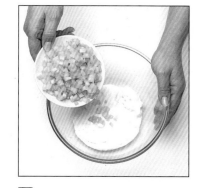

1 Prepare the Coriander Yogurt. Combine all the ingredients in a bowl and season with salt and freshly ground black pepper. Cover and refrigerate until ready to serve.

2 Prepare the marinade. Place all the ingredients in the bowl of a food processor, and process until smooth. Pour into a shallow dish.

3 Freeze the chicken breasts for 5 minutes to firm, then slice in half horizontally. Cut the slices into 2 cm/¾ in strips and add to the marinade. Toss to coat well. Cover and refrigerate for 6–8 hours or overnight.

4 Preheat the grill and line a baking sheet with foil. Using a slotted spoon, remove the chicken from the marinade and arrange the pieces in a single layer on the baking sheet. Scrunch up the chicken slightly so it makes wavy shapes. Grill for 4–5 minutes until brown and just cooked, turning once. Thread 1–2 pieces on to cocktail sticks or short skewers and serve with the yogurt dip.

Glazed Spare Ribs

These delicious sticky ribs are easy to eat with fingers once the little bones are cleaned away at one end to provide "handles".

Makes about 25

INGREDIENTS

1 kg/2¼ lb meaty pork spare ribs, cut into 5 cm/2 in lengths
175 ml/6 fl oz/¾ cup tomato ketchup or mild chilli sauce
30–45 ml/2–3 tbsp soy sauce
30–45 ml/2–3 tbsp clear honey
2 garlic cloves, finely chopped
50 ml/2 fl oz/¼ cup orange juice
1.25 ml/¼ tsp cayenne pepper (or to taste)
1.25 ml/¼ tsp Chinese five-spice powder
1–2 star anise

pork spare ribs

orange juice

soy sauce

star anise

garlic

Chinese five-spice powder

clear honey

ketchup

cayenne pepper

1 Using a small sharp knife, scrape away about 5 mm/¼ in of meat from one end of each tiny spare rib to serve as a little "handle".

2 In a large bowl or shallow baking dish, mix together the ketchup or chilli sauce, soy sauce, honey, garlic, orange juice, cayenne pepper, Chinese five-spice powder and star anise until well blended. Add the ribs and toss to coat. Cover and refrigerate for 6–8 hours or overnight.

3 Preheat the oven to 180°C/350°F/Gas 4. Line a baking sheet with foil and arrange the spare ribs in a single layer, spooning over any remaining marinade.

4 Bake uncovered, basting occasionally, for 1 to 1½ hours, or until the ribs are well browned and glazed. Serve warm or at room temperature.

Sushi-style Tuna Cubes

These tasty tuna cubes are easier to prepare than classic Japanese sushi but retain the same fresh taste.

Makes about 24

INGREDIENTS
675 g/1½ lb fresh tuna steak,
   2 cm/¾ in thick
1 large red pepper, seeded and cut
   into 2 cm/¾ in pieces
sesame seeds, for sprinkling

FOR THE MARINADE
15–30 ml/1–2 tbsp lemon juice
2.5 ml/½ tsp salt
2.5 ml/½ tsp sugar
2.5 ml/½ tsp wasabi paste
120 ml/4 fl oz/½ cup olive or
   vegetable oil

FOR THE SOY DIPPING SAUCE
100 ml/3½ fl oz/2 cups soy sauce
15 ml/1 tbsp rice wine vinegar
5 ml/1 tsp lemon juice
1–2 spring onions, finely chopped
5 ml/1 tsp sugar
2–3 dashes Asian hot chilli oil or hot
   pepper sauce

soy sauce

fresh tuna

coriander   *olive oil*

red pepper   *sesame seeds*

wasabi paste   *lemon juice*   *vinegar*

pepper sauce   *sugar*   *spring onions*

1 Cut the tuna into 2.5 cm/1 in pieces and arrange them in a single layer in a large non-corrosive baking dish.

2 Prepare the marinade. In a small bowl, stir the lemon juice with the salt, sugar and wasabi paste. Slowly whisk in the oil until well blended and slightly creamy. Stir in the coriander. Pour over the tuna cubes and toss to coat. Cover and marinate for about 40 minutes in a cool place.

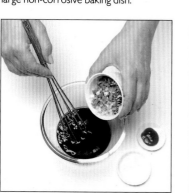

3 Meanwhile, prepare the Soy Dipping Sauce. Combine all the ingredients in a small bowl and stir until well blended. Cover until ready to serve.

4 Preheat the grill and line a baking sheet with foil. Thread a cube of tuna then a piece of pepper on to each skewer and arrange on the baking sheet.

5 Sprinkle with sesame seeds and grill for 3–5 minutes, turning once or twice, until just beginning to colour but still pink inside. Serve with the Soy Dipping Sauce.

COOK'S TIP
Wasabi is a hot, pungent Japanese horseradish available in powder form and as paste in a tube from gourmet and Japanese food shops.

Bombay Prawns

These larger prawns are expensive, so save this dish for a special occasion.

Makes 24

INGREDIENTS

175 ml/6 fl oz/¾ cup olive oil
5 ml/1 tsp ground turmeric (or to taste)
5 ml/1 tsp ground cumin
5 ml/1 tsp garam masala or curry powder
2.5 ml/½ tsp salt
2.5 ml/½ tsp cayenne pepper (or to taste)
juice of 2 limes
24 large uncooked Madagascar or tiger prawns, shelled and deveined, tails attached
coriander leaves, to garnish

limes

shelled prawns

olive oil

turmeric *cumin*

garam masala

coriander

cayenne pepper

1 In a medium-sized bowl, whisk together well the oil, turmeric, cumin, garam masala, salt, cayenne pepper and lime juice.

2 With a small sharp knife, slit three-quarters of the way through each prawn, cutting down the centre back (be careful not to cut right through). Add the prawns to the marinade and allow to stand in a cool place for 40 minutes.

3 Preheat the grill. Arrange the prawns on a foil-lined grill pan in a single layer. Drizzle over a little of the marinade. Grill for about 2 to 3 minutes, until the prawns are glazed and curled. Serve immediately, on cocktail sticks if you like, garnished with coriander leaves.

COOK'S TIP

Wrap the prawn tails in small pieces of foil to prevent them catching and burning under the grill, then remove halfway through cooking. Make sure the prawns are cooked through and test one by cutting in half.

Caramel Cape Gooseberries

These exotic fruits resemble shiny Chinese lanterns when dipped in golden caramel. Their tartness provides a perfect contrast to the sweetness of the coating.

Makes 24

INGREDIENTS
oil, for greasing
24 Cape gooseberries
225 g/8 oz granulated sugar

Cape gooseberries

sugar

1 Lightly oil a small baking sheet. Carefully separate the papery leaves from the fruit of the Cape gooseberry and bend them back behind the berry, twisting them together at the stem.

2 Put the sugar in a small heavy saucepan, sprinkle with 30–45 ml/2–3 tbsp of water and heat over a low heat until the sugar melts, swirling the pan occasionally. Increase the heat to medium and bring to the boil. Boil for 4–5 minutes until the syrup turns a golden caramel colour.

3 Dip the base of the pan in cold water to stop the cooking, then place it in a bowl of warm water so the caramel remains liquid. Be very careful, as the caramel can cause serious burns.

4 Holding each fruit by the papery leaves, carefully dip the berry into the caramel to coat completely. Set each fruit on the prepared baking sheet and allow to cool until hard.